The Essence of a Virtuous Woman

Written By: Bridgette Thornton

The Essence Of A Virtuous Woman

Copyright © 2015 Bridgette N. Thornton

All rights reserved.

No part of this book may be reproduced, copied, stored in a retrieval system transmitted by any means electronically, mechanically, photocopied, recorded or otherwise without the written permission from the author.

Published By: Bridgette Thornton
NuAge JRP. **N**u **U**nderstanding of **A**chieving **G**reater **E**xcellence

ISBN-13: 978-0692499665 (CUSTOM)
ISBN-10: 0692499660
(Bridgette Thornton)

Special Thanks to:
Brian Martin
With Divine Creations Photography LLC.
317-366-2083

Models
Adrienne Hudson
And
Kamaria Thornton-Ford

All scripture quotations have been taken from the King James Version of the Holy Bible.
 Other sayings throughout the book have come from various social media sites like Facebook, Instagram, and Twitter. Some of which are just sayings past down from generation to generation

DEDICATION

The Essence of a Virtuous Woman is dedicated to my amazing children, **Kamaria**, **KamRon**, and **Kaiden**. You three are my reason for breathing. You all keep me grounded and working towards a brighter future. I have had the pleasure of raising you all to be children of the Most High God, and there is no greater reward than seeing you all walk in your purpose and calling at such an early age. I thank you for your love and support and most importantly the laughter. There is never ever a dull moment in the Thornton household and for that I am eternally grateful. I thank you all for making parenting easy as Sunday morning. Keep up the good work mommy loves you.

To my mommy; **Bridgette Wallace**, You are gorgeous, funny as heck, and I love you so much; for always being the voice of reason when I get ready to make a decision that I may later regret. Thank you for being the coolest grandmother in the world to my babies and supporting them in their endeavors. I am so proud of you that I sit in tears and think of all that you have overcome but by the grace of God you are still standing,

To my brother; **Mr. Richard Thornton**, my best friend even when you are being a jerk, I thank you for all of your love and support. Life hasn't always been easy but I have always been able to count on you and your family for everything. There have been plenty of times where you could have said no or not right now but some way somehow you always come through. You have supported every idea I have had from businesses to books and for that I thank you. I am in deed very proud of the man that you have grown up to be. Continue to blaze the trails so that our legacy as Thornton's will continue to live on.

To my sisters; **Shemeka Cornett, Rochelle Thornton, Ramie (Felicia) Jackson**, sister in-law **Grace Watts-Thornton**, I love you ladies and it is a pleasure to be your sister. You all have added so much to my life and the lives of my children and for that I am grateful.

To my auntie; **Kiana Fossett**, I have to say thank you for your support. I have always admired you and your accomplishments. I have learned the true meaning of friendship because of the example that you have shown. You are definitely a Virtuous Woman. I appreciate you taking care of our family with grace and sophistication.

To my Grandparents; **Carolyn Darden** and **Tommy Fossett**, Granny and Granddaddy I love you two so very much. I appreciate all that you have added to my life and the lives of my children. Whenever I need a good laugh I can always count on Granny to give it to me. And Grandddaddy I appreciate the fight in you. And great sense of humor. Thank you.

To my God- Grandparents; **Bernice** and **Julius Jones** you two have been my example of what marriage should be. I watch you two still in love after 58 years it's like you are still just as in love today as you were back then. I thank you for always supporting me and my family through all of life's marvelous occasions. And praying for me when I didn't have enough sense to pray for myself

To my Pastors; **Apostle Jacqueline E. Powell** and **Pastor Margaret Means** and the whole Augusta Christian Church Family and Powerhouse International Ministries located at 3445 W. 71st. St. Indianapolis IN. thank you all for your continued support, prayer, and motivation. I thank you for your spiritual covering and guidance. Being taught in an Apostolic Training Center has made this Christian walk very fulfilling. Thank you.

To Pastor **Michael E. Rutledge;** and my Mt. Ararat Baptist Church family located at 5801 W. Montgomery Rd. Houston TX. Thank you all for your continued support and prayers. You all have made living in Houston very fulfilling and memorable.

To my friends,

Falisha Brightwell, for 23 years you have been there for me ride or die thick as thieves my sister, I am so proud of the woman you have grown to be. We may not always see eye to eye but at the end of the day I know I can count on you and your family to be there when the dust settles. I love you lady.

Rotunda Montgomery, I have had the pleasure of being your best friend and having you as mine for the past 9 years. Who would have ever thought that something so special and wonderful could have come from Hurricane Katrina? God blew you all the way north during a time when we would need each other the most. I thank you for allowing me and my family to be a part of yours. You have made it through the storm sis and the best is definitely yet to come. I love you and appreciate your friendship.

Melissa Jones, We have been best friends for 15 years. You have opened my eyes to so many possibilities and an undying love for traveling. Because of you I have had an opportunity to see parts of the world I hadn't even imagined would happen until after retirement, I am so proud of you and the things that you have accomplished in this lifetime are simply breathtaking, I keep a bag packed and ready go!!!!

Kizzy Hayes, What can I say you are indeed my sister, my friend, my business partner, I mean the list just goes on. You always have a way of making it all make sense and for your friendship I thank you for all of your encouragement and support not just from a personal aspect but, from a business as well. Divas in Red Outreach Ministry Inc. would not be as strong as it is today without your unfailing contributions and efforts.

Gina Hawkins, my friend and business partner, I just love you so much. Divas in Red Outreach Ministry Inc. could not continue on the level of excellence without your skills, your support, and the ability to network like no other. I appreciate all of the hard work you do for us and for that I am eternally grateful.

Edmond Banks I just smile to myself every time I say your name. We have been friends for 21 years easy. I love you so much and the amazing man you have grown to become I know your parents are smiling down on you in shear amazement. One particular gesture that you made, when I was what 15 years old, I have carried with me throughout life. I stole Falisha's car barely able to drive might I add and in the snow. I drove clear across town to see you. I asked you for some money. I have no clue why I did but I did.

You smiled that big beautiful smile and said wait here. You took off into the house. When you returned to the car you handed me an application. I still crack up laughing every time I think about how pissed off I was at you. Then to get back to Falisha's only for her to throw a gallon of cold water on me for taking her car while she was sleep. Because of that gesture I make it a point to work hard as I possibly can so I wouldn't have to depend on a man again. So I thank you for that. Because of you I have one heck of a work ethic,

To **Monique Wagner**, and **Kelleen Robertson**, thank you ladies for allowing me and my family to be a small part of your life. Each friendship developed over this lifespan I hold dear. And no matter where this life takes us just know that I appreciate you all so much and it has certainly been a pleasure.

To **all of my Divas in Red** with Divas in Red Outreach Ministry Inc. from the Divas to the parents the volunteers and my Board of Directors. To all of you who make my job as Founder and CEO possible. I enjoy working with you all and look forward to the next level of success granted by God. There is a reason we are all together working together laughing together and changing lives together. Each one of you play an amazing role in making sure we give back in way that can only be done Diva Style. You all are my family. I thank you for the ideas, the support, and continued effort in my vision to change the world one diva at a time.

And last but certainly not least to **all of my readers**, thank you for allowing me to bless you with my gift of poetry. You all are the reason I continue to write, with each book you buy not only are you getting a great read but you are contributing to the support of children suffering from Cerebral Palsy. With each book sold a percentage will be donated to different agencies who offer support for those children and their families. So again I say thank you.

So again The Essence of a Virtuous Woman is dedicated to all of you. Because without your support I wouldn't be able to bring you such an outstanding book I pray that you enjoy reading it as much as I enjoyed writing it.

Note to Readers,

I am so pleased to present to you The Essence of a Virtuous Woman. Many of you are familiar with my style of storytelling. As an author and Poet I fuse the two to bring real life situations and struggles to the fore front. A lot of these characters are just like you or me or Sister so and so. We all know someone who has been through; or even still going through similar situations. My prayer is that you read my work and relate. Take something positive away from it that may help you to understand and have compassion for the next person. Or even find hope and aspiration within your own circumstance.

We all have a story to tell. None of us are perfect but knowing that you are not alone can bring not only comfort but also joy and hope. But most importantly, it can bring healing. I invite you to lose yourself in the midst of these pages. Understand that there are scenes throughout the pages of this book that may be detailed as a bit vulgar but yet tasteful. I would ask that you read with an open heart and mind. **Viewer discretion is advised.**

There are some sexually explicit content because of the nature of this book, however each testimony in real life does not usually come with a sensor. But because I try to focus on real life situations I paint the picture vividly.
I give it to you as it comes to me in raw form.

So as you journey through the lives of these characters, be at peace. Yes these are characters, and some situations have truly come from individuals that I have crossed paths with, who have endured each struggle first hand. And others were definitely my imagination running wild. But either way be prepared to venture off into the world of The Essence of a Virtuous Woman.

Thank you all for your continued support and of course if you haven't gotten your copy of **The UnMasking of Me** I suggest you do so. Not because I am the author but because it too is an awesome read, or so I'm told, God Bless you and may you continue to live in Faith, Love, Laughter, and Hope.

Bridgette Thornton

Table of Contents

~Chapter 1~

Title of Poem	**Page #**
1. **The Essence of a Virtuous Woman**	12
2. Beautiful	17
3. Invisible	19
4. **But You Are a Queen Though**	21
5. Silence	29

~Chapter 2~

6. **She's All Gone Now**	32
7. A Good Thing Gone	46
8. When it's Time to Boot Up, Men Listen Up	49
9. He Can Be Saved	51

~Chapter 3~

10. Fed up   55

11. I Love Me Enough   62

12. Ok So I Date   64

13. How Do You Love Someone without First Loving Yourself   66

14. **Sweet Dreams**   69

~Chapter 4~

15. Get Low   74

16. Thinking Back   78

17. My Mother   82

18. Senior Dream Team   85

19. Surrender   87

~Chapter 5~

20. If Jesus Wrote You a Letter Responding To Your Prayer	93
21. Hood Love	96
22. I See	108
23. Mary Magdalene	110

~Excerpts from the UnMasking of Me~

24. The UnMasking Of Me	112
25. Forgiveness	115
26. Important Scriptures to Know	118
27. Emergency Contact Information and Websites	122
28. About The Author	125
29. Photo Gallery	126

THE ESSENCE OF A VIRTUOUS WOMAN

The essence of a virtuous woman
Is not determined by the color of her skin
But by the grace of God when she was custom made
Prior to her mother's womb
She has the ability to love on a level
That can't be explained
She has the patience of Job, and the Wisdom of Solomon
And knows how to smile while in pain

The essence of a virtuous woman
Was exposed when she conceived
And brought forth life you see
When she not only raises her children
But the children in her family and community

Her essence can be seen from miles away
When she humbles herself before God
So that even for you she can pray

Her essence can be found in the way she dresses herself
You won't see the breast she used
To nurture her child through her blouse

You won't see the belly that once housed
The children you see today
But she's clothed in dignity, and respect,
And she carries herself in such a way
That, even those who know her story
And in spite of her mistakes will still say,

She has just a little bit of pride
And whole lot of favor and faith
And because the God she serves is true,
For her He has always made a way

The essence of a virtuous woman

The Essence Of A Virtuous Woman

Is not found in the money she makes
But in the community service and in the charity
And the tithes that she pays

It's in the bills that get paid on time
Or before they are due
It's in the savings and preparation
For her children's future

Her essence
Is not found in the car she drives
But in the transportation to and from
The Doctor appointments, when her neighbors need a ride.

It's not found in the home she resides in
But it's in the pull out couch where many have slept
When she had to take them in

It's not determined by the man that she dates
But in the man she forgave over and over again
After all of his hurtful mistakes

The essence of a virtuous woman
Can be seen and felt for many years to come
In the friendship of those whose secrets she has kept
Between her and God

Her essence
Can be heard out loud without her speaking a word
It can be found in her actions
Because those speak louder than words

It can be heard in shear silence
Because she knows how to be quiet
And simply pray instead of gossip

Her essence is seen in her ability to multiply too
While making do with what little she has
There is still enough to feed you

It can be seen from generations to come
Because she has left and inheritance
For her loved ones

The essence of a virtuous woman
Has always been visible even today
If you give her sperm she in return
Will give you a beautiful baby

But the essence of a virtuous man
Will allow him to be separated from the boys
Because while boys make babies
Real men raise their children and yours
By teaching, loving, bonding,
And disciplining them as real men do

Her essence can be found in the house you give
Because in return she will give you a home
To raise your family in

The essence of a virtuous man
Will build that home for you all to reside in
However a boy will play house,
He will get in where he can fit in.

The essence of a virtuous man
Will attract the essence of a virtuous woman,
This is why he will make her his wife
While boys like to shack up with a baby mama
With no intentions of marriage in his life

Her essence
Can be found in the groceries you give
Because in return now you get plenty
Of home cooked meals

It can be found in the smile that you give
Because in return she will give you her heart

And in hers you will always live

The essence of a virtuous man
Will not allow him to be disrespectful or harm you
Because of the fear of God
He knows your worth and will cherish you

Her essence
Is not predicated on your emotions
Because she is still a woman
And real women have side effects

She is allergic to bull crap and things that make no sense
Like telling lies when the truth is really all she expects?

The essence of a virtuous man
Will tell you the truth even if it hurts
He has enough sense to be honest
Because he values your trust

The side effects of a virtuous woman is
Simply the fact that she is allergic to being broke
She is not lazy and has ambition and drive
She dreams big and enjoys a good joke

She has no problem with helping those
Who want to help themselves do better
Although she won't be taken advantage of
Nor will she ever settle

The essence of a virtuous woman
Is found in her attitude because failure is not an option
She explores every opportunity
Or door that may have been opened

While boys invent new excuses
To justify their failures
The essence of a virtuous man
Will produce strategies for his success

To ensure the needs of
His virtuous woman and family are met

Boys look for someone to take care of them
While virtuous men look for a virtuous woman
To take care of while
Boys seek popularity
Virtuous men demand respect and know how to give it.

So I say this all to say to both women and men,
Know who you are in Christ because that's what matters in the end.
By knowing you are a child of God
And the essence of Christ should be seen everyday
In not only your attitude but in your actions,
In your decisions and in the choices you make.

Nobody is perfect nor will we ever be.
However knowing your sheer essence
Will keep you from lacking

Rather it be in love or laughter
In your tears while happy or even sad
The essence of a child of God trumps it all in the end.

Treat people the way you want to be treated
And forgive as often as you breathe
I guarantee that God will smile down on you
And meet more than just your needs.

Beautiful

The **B** in Beautiful is for the **Boldness** we should all have.
To share the Word of God to those who are happy as well as sad.

The **E** is for **Everlasting life**, which God has promised us.
A place where we can live eternally, where we don't have
To fight or fuss.

The **A** is for the **Anointing** that destroys the yolk.
The anointing that saves and sets us apart,
From all the average folks

The **U** is for **Understanding**, because God knows our hearts
By faith we trust in him and through mercy we have a fresh start.

The **T** is for the **Trust** but not in man at all,
But trusting in the Lord our God
And on His Word be prepared to stand tall.

The **I** is for **Inherit**, because we were born to a King.
We were adopted into royalty so we have access to everything.

The **F** is for **Faithful** which his track record proves.
There is not another, who can do, half the things
That God has promised to do.

The **U** is for **Unity** which is how we all must be.
We are the body of Christ and the spirit of division
Shouldn't be

The **L** is for **Love**. God's greatest gift to man.
He died and shed his pure blood
So that we may live instead

So each time you look into the mirror,
And a reflection looks back.

Keep in mind you are **BEAUTIFUL** and there is nothing You have to lack.

Invisible

There is someone out there living in a home filled with fear.
Praying that one day someone would wipe away their tears.

He or she may be filled with doubt,
Trying to figure out what life is really about.
You may have never noticed how
Quiet they can be.
Whenever someone says to them
It's ok just trust me.
Or maybe when they laugh just to keep from crying;
Knowing deep inside their soul is really dying.

But these are the people who need that extra love.
Some special attention, a warm smile or maybe a hug
They need to know that everything will be alright.
And that Jesus died for their sins and He can make everything right.

But sometimes we are so caught up on things that don't matter.
Never stopping to think how many lives are being shattered.

Now don't get me wrong
We all have done this.
But its time out for all the foolishness;
Because it's important to see beyond the surface,
And start living our lives
As if we have purpose.

And that's because it does
God created us from dust
So that we could know His love;

It's about time for us to take a stand as a people,
And love one another no matter the season.

Every one of us has a story to tell.

While searching for that one thing
To make us feel.
Good all over inside and out.
And experience life without having doubts.

About why God made us just the way we are,
Maybe He made a mistake or are we really a star?
God loves you this you should know.
Because He created you for a season
Just ask him to show
You what He is truly about?
I guarantee through praise He will definitely show out.

The Essence Of A Virtuous Woman

But You Are a Queen Though

How was I supposed to know you were Queen?
Heck I don't think that you even knew.
Seeing how you always dressing like you're the badest chick
I see your breast, your legs, your thighs and your hips.
In all of the Facebook, Twitter, and Instagram pics
But you are a Queen though.

How am I supposed to know?
Because each time I call at 2 or 3 in the morning you pick up.
And say "What's Up"?
Not once did you go off about me calling you too late.
I tell you I'm about to slide through
And your response is okay.
But you are a Queen though?

Yet you smoke weed, pop pills and snort powder,
Get your welfare, food stamps and live in public housing.
But you are a Queen though?

I didn't even have to wine you or dine you.
No standards had to be met at all.
No background checks, no employment verified
Not even a credit check.
But you are a Queen though.

Not once did you ask if I ever had or do I have an STD.
Or when was the last time I have been tested for AIDS or HIV?
Not one time did you ever suggest that I use a Rubber?
Although I suggested you do my buddy since you claim you love me.
But you are a Queen though

How was I supposed to know when your kid's child support money comes in

You go run and spend that dough quick,
But not on your kids
But on that quick weave, and your nails so you can imitate what
A real queen is Hmmm.
But you are a Queen though.

Now it's all really true, you are indeed a queen though.
Falling from your rightful place on your throne
At that very moment your child hood was shattered by no fault of
your own.
But by the original queen of her throne in your home

But you call her mommy.
Mommy has hurt you in ways that no child should ever have to
endure.
Instead of protecting you from him, they should have protected
you from her
But you are a Queen though.

You see there is a reason you started having sex at the age of nine.
You were a product of your environment
Raised amongst women who themselves had no clue of their
strength.
Had no clue that they too were queens
So to raise one would have been impossible or so it seems.
But you are a Queen though.

These women have embedded in your head
That nothing comes for free.
Not one woman in your family has ever been married.
Now the decision to have sex at the age of nine
Was not your own.
Your mother thought for some perverse reason
That it was about your time.

To make you comfortable and teach you the ropes
Mommy wanted to teach you what to expect first
So when the time came it wouldn't hurt.
But you are a Queen though.

The Essence Of A Virtuous Woman

She told you to come here.
Now mommy's job is to protect pretty little girls
From the big bad men
But I am about to show you what happens when
Mommies are plagued with the spirit of perversion
She filled the tub with bubbles.
But you are a Queen though

She told you to get in and handed you a Seagram's wine cooler in a glass.
Now at the age of nine you figured it was only juice in a glass
No way was mommy really going to let you drink.
So as you handed it back to her she said "it's ok" and insisted you just drink.
But you are a Queen though

So, like a good little girl you laid back and drank it until it was gone.
Once you were done your mommy told you to wash up and don't be too long.
When you got out the tub mommy dried you off
And rubbed lotion all over your body, even between the cheeks of your butt
Real soft and gentle she wasn't being rough.
But you a Queen Though

Now usually you do it all by yourself
Generally you would stand up
Mommy says yes you are a big girl now.
But she applied the lotion different this time,
Now this time she told you to lie down.
But you are a Queen though

Now mommy told you to close your eyes as tight as you can
Feeling a little dizzy you never even noticed mommies hand.
"Maybe mommy is putting on my under pants",
You hear mommy humming and smell her perfume
Not once did you ever hear anyone else enter the room.

Bridgette N. Thornton

But you are a Queen though

You felt the hands on your chest
Still pretty dizzy and eyes shut
You hear mommy say its okay baby just rest.
But how can you when you feel something wet and warm down there
And a sensation between your legs that no child should ever feel

You think this can't be mommy not with her mouth on me
And so afraid to open your eyes just to peek
So finally after looking just a little your heart skipped a beat.
To see that yes it is your mommy
With her face between your knees
But you are a Queen though

As the tears roll down your cheeks you turn your head to the right
And see a grown man with a camera and a big bright light
Still so dizzy, this has got to be a dream.
This is supposed to be my mommy.
But you are a Queen though

Not sure how to feel you can't help but just lay there and cry
After a while your body went limp
Although clearly you could still feel every bit of it
You feel mommy insert what looked to be a male's penis
Only purple down there
The harder you cried the deeper she went
To weak and drugged up to fight back
Having to endure the humiliation of molestation in front of a camera
And strangers
But you are a Queen though.

Now although these sick sexual acts went from bad to worst.
When mommy made you dance and sleep with men for money
You thought for sure you'd be in the back of a Hurst.

Sometimes they would just pay to watch mommy bathe you

The Essence Of A Virtuous Woman

They pay her in drugs in alcohol so that they could have their way with you
But you are a Queen though

At such a small fragile age all the drugs and sex made you very sick
You ended up in the hospital and told that you were an addict.
An addict to sex, drugs, and money although you can barely read or write
You have been a childhood sex slave for five years and had a heck of a life
But you are a Queen though

So now at fourteen you are in and out of rehabs and foster cares too.
You hate men and women and you hate those who hate you.
With the molestation that you suffered at the hands of your mother
Had you terrified of one day becoming a mother

But as you got older you found it hard to deal and relate to life
You figured you of all people didn't really deserve a good life
But you are a Queen though

Now if a man or a woman can make you happy then so be it
You wanted the finer things in life like the Louie, the Prada and let's not forget the Gucci.
It didn't matter how you got it or who bought it.
But you are a Queen though

So now you wear the label of being Bi-Sexual cause you used what you had
To get what you wanted and both men and women were eager to buy.
Heck let you tell it mommy did you a favor
By teaching you the game at an early age
Now you are the very best at what you do
You have been known to drive a crazy person sane.
But you are a Queen though

You don't seem to care, no emotions or attachments
No nothing at all
You did everything under the sun
When that money called
But you are a Queen though

Finally you get pregnant and honestly,
You didn't think that could happen
Since you stayed so high that the sperm
Would have had to swim through paraphernalia

But it's cool because no way you would keep it
To far along for an abortion
So an adoption it is
No drugs no sex just a minor set back
For a few months or so
Once the baby arrived the script was flipped
And you couldn't help but want to see this little baby grow.
But you are a Queen though

Why couldn't you be a good mother?
Better than the one you had.
Why couldn't you work like normal people?
Because you didn't possess the skills normal people had.
But you are a Queen though

Now after three children and no job or education
You live in subsidized housing
Cause the state helps to pay for your rehabilitation.

Now I know your wondering will this be a happy ending?
Does she find Jesus and get delivered?
Maybe a church home that helps meet her spiritual edification
And teach her biblical revelation?

Or does a sister or brother come to save her
From a week long crack binge
In the trap house with the homies
Or does she get her act together and share her testimony?

The Essence Of A Virtuous Woman

But what you will soon find out is that I can't.
I can't tell you how the story will end for a Queen
I surely would if I could
However this Queen has yet to discover her royally priesthood
Because she is still trapped in the hood

Meaning poverty stricken being born
Into a generation plagued with the spirit of perversion,
The spirit of addiction Read about them in the scriptures.

The spirit of lust, and of lasciviousness,
The spirit of depression and rejection
The spirit of fornication just to name a few
She has been suffering with all these demons her whole
Life and yet had no clue

This is the same Queen that you sit and talk bad about
You turn your noses up at her and make assumptions about,
What she should or shouldn't be doing with her life
Not realizing it's not a choice for her it's all she knows so to her it is right

By not having spiritual discernment, to see each demon
That occupied her flesh
Causing so much strife and pain in her life
With the ultimate goal being death

Not fully understanding that each demon
Had a legal right to be
Ephesians is a great place to read.
Where the spirit of the Lord is there is light and darkness has to flee
They had a legal right to occupy that space because not once has this Queen ever confessed her love for Christ.
So that she can be set free.
She would have had to be reborn again to live in liberty

You sit and talk about her instead of trying to help her out

You can't stand to see her coming so you purposely change your route.

But she is a Queen though
She has to realize her worth she can be your neighbor, your sister, your cousin and for some of you she is your mother.
Be careful with whom you cast judgment lest you too be judged

And not to mention he who is without sin
Let him cast the first stone.
You never know what a person is going through.
God has called each of us to be the light of the world. And to love

Each other as He loves us. Period point blank
So please keep in mind the next time you point one finger at someone
You have three more pointing back at you.

Silence

Some folks have got the game all mixed up.
They seem to think its ok to send you through
Unnecessary stuff

We have all been taught if someone hits you
Then it's ok to hit them back
So where in the rules does it say
It's ok to hit the ones you love
across the face, or even in the back?

Abuse is such a sneaky little something
And if you're not careful it will show up
Through anger and insecurities
Even having a low self-esteem,
Will have you questioning someone's trust;

There is never an excuse to make it all seem right
Don't blame it on the drugs or the drink
Or how you have had such a messed up life

At some point we should take responsibility for our own actions.
Going through life like your reading closed captions.

It usually starts with the nit picking.
Going back and forth with one another
Usually something petty like
Baby daddy's and mothers.

Always looking for an easy target to talk about;
Although the talking always escalates into yelling
and then to shouting.

But eventually hollering isn't working
You can't seem to get your point across.

Bridgette N. Thornton

So you push and you shove and before you know it
You have slapped her in the mouth.

You're passed the name calling, her self-esteem is low
She loses more of herself
With each punch and each blow

She's belittled because now she has to beg
And plead with a monster.
Who loves to punch her in the head
And leave bruises on her legs.

She answers to every foul name in the book.
While making sure to take care of the kids,
She still has to clean and cook.

Even while her head is still hurting from the night before,
When he came home drunk and drug across the bedroom floor

Her friends say to leave him
But what do they know?
He pays all the bills and takes good care of the kids so

Everybody goes through it besides he is just stressed
Maybe if she lost a little weight then just maybe
They will fight a little less.

Or so she says you see excuses are what she has grown accustomed too.
"Cover Girl" make-up to hide all of her bruises
It took her so long to reveal the abuse to another
Afraid of what people what say or if they would judge her.

She married her husband in an attempt to find true love herself
However falling in love with a stranger
Kept her holding on to what was left.
She didn't realize that she'd gone about things all wrong
Biblically a man who finds a wife finds a good thing
However she never called.

On the name of God to guide her before it began
Now she suffering in silence because
She really loves him.

She watched her mom, step mom, cousins and friends
Go through the same thing with these men
At some point we have to say enough and be gone.

Instead of continuing the generational curses to
that contaminate
Our homes
What we fail to realize is abuse it's just that
Rather your hitting or punching, name calling or neglect.

Just know it's not acceptable and you have to want more
Instead of suffering with a man
Who you should have kicked out the door

She's All Gone Now

Alyssa spent a lifetime focused on her career.
Over achieving in every aspect,
Hit every goal that was set
All praises she would hear.

So determined to make a life
Where she could extend a helping hand
She watched her mother struggle for so long
Wasn't sure how she could stand.

She knew she didn't want welfare, food stamps,
Or social security checks
She wanted to live in a big house, and drive a Benz
Or maybe even a Lexus.

Alyssa wanted her own company
Didn't want to work for anyone
Public Service of some sort,
Wanted to leave a legacy when she was done

She made it through school great grades and all
Managed to keep her virginity
Boys couldn't get close at all.

Off to college she was starting to find her way
Was sure of herself so she chose not to date
Graduation came quick because she stayed in the books
Volunteering her time was also a great look

So needless to say her own company was started
She was reaching out to the community
Because she wanted to help everybody

Very successful in life

The Essence Of A Virtuous Woman

She didn't have a care in the world at all
She was a beautiful sistah with a mocha caramel complexion
Who was about to take a hard fall

One evening after a long hard day at work,
And way too tired to cook
She stopped at the little restaurant on her way home
Just down past the brook

She sat in her usual seat, kind of off to the back.
Cozy and comfortable so she could just relax
Placed her order for some baked chicken, mac and cheese,
Collard greens and a slice of sweet potato pie
Reminded her of Granny's kitchen
On Sunday after church my, my, my

While waiting on her order she opens her book to read.
When out of the corner of her eye she could see.
To say that he was tall, dark, and handsome
Sounds just like a cliché
But this man here was different
In every single way

David had confidence and pride
And well-groomed to say the least
He hung that Armani suite like
Morris Chestnut was a beast

He had a smile that could melt and turn lava ice cold.
He had beautiful gray eyes that had a story to be told.
He walked as if there laid a trail of rose petals at his feet.
Cautious erythematic steps like he was in no hurry to get to his seat.

As she watches from across the room
He finally notices her all alone.
The most beautiful woman on the earth
Made him want to sing her a song

It didn't matter if he looked foolish or not
He would be willing to dance the jig
In the middle of the parking lot
If it meant she would keep smiling non stop

Something about her physique or maybe her graceful poise
That caught his undivided attention he felt like a little boy.
With his first crush, not knowing what to say
And before he knew it he was at her table
Asking about her day

They enjoyed polite conversation with one another
A little eating, a little drinking, and a whole lot of flirting
Now here she is having never been on a date.
Conversing with this stranger she thought for sure
Would be her soul mate.

After dinner they exchanged numbers and planned to meet again
She felt like she was the lead in a movie but then,
After a while of talking, texting, emailing and such
The conversation about sex had finally come up

He would tell her that he wanted to make love to her
But she simply said no.
Although she wanted him to but
She wanted to wait until marriage so,

Before she knew it days had turned into weeks
And those weeks into months
The relationship was progressing with lots of love
And plenty of lust

So David pops the question seeing how life was too short
This was so true.
He wanted to make her his wife and couldn't wait
For Alyssa to say I do.

The wedding was gorgeous like a dream come true.
The honeymoon was even better

The Essence Of A Virtuous Woman

She thought she was slow dancing on the moon.

Because for the first time she was being made love too
Held close while tears escaped her eyes
All she could hear him say was baby I love you.

So you would think she had her happily ever after
But that's a far stretch from the truth.
All hell seemed to break loose
After she said I do.

The first few months it was all still new
But then it's like he was changing
And there was nothing she could do.

It seemed like the sex got rougher
and stranger at the same time
Now David was doing things that simply blew her mind.

She was past deep in love and for her husband
He could have it all.
She wanted to please him in every area
She would run whenever he'd call.

After the first year it seemed that making love wasn't an option
Several times a day like clockwork
She was always happy and even after arguing they could make up.
With some kinky little toy, some lingerie and chocolate.

What was this man doing that had her losing her mind?
Because before she knew it, she was no longer on her grind.
Then one day the sex just stopped
He was coming in from working late
And on the couch is where he flopped.

Always making excuses as to why he wasn't in the mood
Left her in bed all alone
And to top it all off he was being rude.
So after a while of the same old thing

Bridgette N. Thornton

She asks him point blank
"Should she take off this ring"?

Of course he says "no" He's got a lot on his plate.
Just need her to understand that he loves her
But it's getting late

Still not satisfied and confused even the more,
She went back to bed after slamming the bedroom door

After a while she's thinking he is such a cheating bastard in deed
Ready to go toe to toe with the woman,
Who had been satisfying her husband's needs.

But what she will soon discover is that honesty
Is not always the best policy.
She was in love with a stranger who was playing
A very deadly game
But eventually the puzzle unfolds and her life will soon change.

Now he knew it was only a matter of time
Before she would give up.
On listening to the crock of bull crap
He had managed to cook up.

He had to think quick especially since things
Were about to hit the fan.
So used to having his cake and eating it too
He thought just like most men.

His secret lifestyle had started to catch up
And even get the best of him.
Running out of excuses no longer having the ability
To be creative with them.

Now she's thinking and thinking
With no logical explanation for his behavior.
She's been through the cell phone, emails, and his letters.

Looking for signs or something to tell her she was wrong
And that her husband had been faithful all along.
One morning she woke up not feeling good at all
And nothing to do
Coughing and a major fever
Too sick to even move.

She made her some hot tea
But was wishing it was Theraflu.
She used cough drops, heating pads
Yet nothing seemed to work
After all she had done it all seemed
To be getting worst.

Finally she made her a doctor's appointment
And when he drew her blood
He asked if there had been a chance
That she could possibly had been exposed.

To HIV or Aids? Were condoms being used on a regular?
She thought to herself DANG that was bold
Her mouth hung open in shock she says, "I only have a cold".

He told her of the tests she should take
And how not knowing was half the battle,
But everyone should still be tested
Especially if you've been sexually active.

She had her pap smear and blood was drew
She was so nervous she didn't know what to do
She was scared and got to thinking
Well plotting is more like it
About all the things she would do
If that test came back positive.

But while comforting herself through her memories
Of the wonderful life she had lived.
Married to her first love, great family, and thriving career.

There was no way she could have been exposed
Since drugs she didn't do.
Her husband was too deep in love with her
And she loved him too.

Now back to him he's pacing the floor
Contemplating his next move
Because clearly he had been a whore.

Now let's rewind his story back before they met
What he has failed to tell his wife
Is that he has also failed his test.

You see the price he paid for his career was heavy in the game
He was a part of an elite group of men
Prominent with fortune and fame.

This secret society of brotherly love
Was way more that he had bargained for
In order to be initiated he had to have fun
In his "back door,"

Several men all in a room although poker
Was not the choice at hand.
All these men enjoyed one another
While having sex with other men.

Now in his eyes he wasn't gay
It was only business
Just in a different sort of way.

But if his wife found out then his marriage would be through.
Simply because he had a secret that only he and the elite knew
However what he didn't know is that everyone
Was not safe
They were not to become intimate with other males
Outside the Safe.

Now the Safe was like a lodge where the men usually met

The Essence Of A Virtuous Woman

Sometimes once or twice a month
To handle their secret business.

Apparently the traitor had a fetish for male prostitutes
Slipped up one day and no protection was used
And well you get the picture.

Now he's fighting demons from all his impurities
Unable to sleep at night
He wakes up screaming from bad dreams and
And even awful sights.

He was tricked into the safe with promises of wealth
A chance to live a full life with
The help of someone else.
So out of revenge and despite the harm
When he found out he was positive with HIV
He felt he had been wronged.

So after careful planning he managed to sleep
With each man in the Safe.
Over a two week period and unprotected sex, his hate
Had soon turned into rage.

Now just imagine if all men who were involved
All had wives at home
Unaware of the games being played
After their husbands had left home.

Now back to Alyssa awaiting her test results,
Was about to find out the love of her life
Was just a hoax.

She steps into the tiny room with sterile white walls
Not knowing what to expect.
And before she knew it the tears began to fall.

After waiting for what seemed to be an eternity
Dr. Thomas walks in with the news that

To her was worse than HIV.

She had been diagnosed with having full blown AIDS
She blacked out while praying this was a horrible dream.
That she was unable to awake from for days.

After coming too she seemed extremely numb
Trying to figure out how she could have been so dumb
How could this be? There has to be some sort of mistake.
Check and recheck the test results
For goodness sakes.

"How do I overcome this"? Was the first question she asked,
Then of course came the fury she wanted to kill his a**.
She drove and drove trying to make sense of this mess.
What did she ever do to deserve such a harsh punishment?

Nothing was making sense
None of it could add up.
Her husband had a lot to explain
She felt so messed up.

She wanted to pray but didn't feel God even cared a little bit.
He couldn't possibly love her she felt cursed,
She needed a wall so she could run her car through it.

But not before she offed her husband
With a death sentence on her hands
There was no way he could explain it.

So finally she pulls up at home
And just as she suspects
Her husband was gone.

She pulled her a glass of wine
And at the table she just sat.
Sitting and contemplating on how he would react.

Better yet, how she would be calm, understanding

And how she wouldn't scream.
But eventually that all changed when
He popped up on the scene.

She sat with her legs crossed, with her glass of wine in hand
Thinking to herself
I'm going to kill this man.

He says, "Hey baby how was your day"?
She smiles politely and says.
"I've had an interesting day".

She told him, "to have a seat
Cause they really needed to talk like right now"
He said, "Sure babe what's up"
She says, "Sit yourself down",

He starts smiling and says, "I must be in trouble
Because you don't even drink"
She says, "Is there something you need to tell me"?
He says, "No"
She says, "THINK".

She said, "I'm going to ask you again
But this time I want the truth
Before I get up out this chair,
And all hell will break loose",

He sits straight up and says, "What's really going on?
I've been at work all day
Just tell me what's wrong
So we can move on",

He says, "I'm tired can this wait until in the morning
After we've had some sleep and then we can talk about it
Whatever the problem is I'm sure we can fix it
But not while your upset and drinking liquor".

She says, "You know what baby

As always you're right.
Go on in the room and relax alright,

Let me run you some bath water so you can relax a little while
Then I'll fix you some dinner," and then she just smiled.
He agrees and off to the room he went
Singing as he walked while she was still sipping.

Alyssa stands up and makes her way to the bathroom.
To run his water and even added bubbles
And told him his water would be ready soon.

Now off to the kitchen to make dinner as she promised him.
Grilled chicken, salad, garlic bread just enough for him;
She went back into the bathroom where David sat in the tub
She kneeled down and washed him up
And gave him a real good back rub.

When she was done she helped him out and into his robe
Walked him into the bedroom
Where his chicken was hot
And his salad was cold.

After he ate, she told him, "That she needed to be made love to
That she was stressed out and that he needed her too".
There was no way he could tell her no
Especially not tonight
After all she was upset and he had just avoided a fight.

So he agrees with her and disrobes without a care in the world.
She gets her toy box from the closet and pulls up a chair.
As she goes through the box she removes four sets of handcuffs.
His eyes light up as he says,
"Wow babe a little rough"?

She smiled coldly and nodded her head
With her cuffs in hand she climbs in the bed.
And one by one she cuffed his hands and his legs
To the headboard and foot posts

The Essence Of A Virtuous Woman

At the bottom of the bed

As he lay there naked she hops off of the bed
Walks into the kitchen and grabbed the sharpest knife
Cause she wanted him dead.

Although the knife was only for the visual effect
She had her razor tucked away inside her cleavage.
With the knife behind her back and grits boiling on the stove
She made her way back in the room
To hear the lies as they unfold.

She asks him again, "is there something you need to tell me"?
He's in total shock because clearly he's helpless.
Before he could answer she removes the paper from her drawer
That confirms she has a disease that no man could cure.

She asked him to explain and that he better do it quick:
Unless she would indeed chop off his precious penis
He starts to cry when he realizes she is for real
Or either crazy and insane
With a knife in one hand ready to dismember his manhood
On this particular day

She can't understand him through all of his pitiful crying,
So she goes back to the hot grits
Cause she has no time for his lying

She began to pour a little bit at a time,
From his face to his neck and on down to his waistline
He's talking fast but he's stuttering she could hear him say
That "he just found out himself, just the other day"

Now this made her madder so she dumped all the grits
Dead smack on his entire penis
He's screaming and yelling and crying a bit
Had the nerve to be angry and called her a Bi**h

Now this only made matters much worse

Cause out of her cleavage she pulled out her razor
And before it was all over she had is manhood in one hand
The razor in the other and he was passed out on the bed

She puked where she stood with no remorse at all
This trifling man deserved every ounce of pain he got
Every bit of it all

She didn't realize that there was banging at the door
And before she could blink
The police had her handcuffed on the floor.

Unable to explain what she had done you see
Because nothing was worse than the fact
That she had to live with AIDS and not HIV.
He was rushed off to the hospital and she was taken to jail
To ashamed to talk about it
Not enough energy to even pray about it.

Her story was on every news station
And radio station too
It caught the eyes of some folks who wanted to help her too.

They wrote letters and raised funds
For a lawyer in her defense
Because clearly she was the victim in all of this

By the time she got in front of a judge who heard her case
Not a jury of her own peers could convict her in that place.
She was released from jail with a different outlook on life
With so many encouraging letters that uplifted her life.

When she got home to pack up her things
She had a check for 50 million dollars from the elite
To cover all of her bills and medical expenses

Now don't get it twisted they all had been tested
But not concerned with the results
They were preparing themselves for the absolute worst.

The Essence Of A Virtuous Woman

Alyssa was back in church and believing God for her healing
She definitely was a firm believer in miracles.
As far as her husband she divorced him of course
And the man who started this mess confessed
And in a prison is where he sat.

Now Alyssa is teaching others about the importance of the test
That is her way of coping and outreaching through her business.
She has forgiven him but however she may never be the same
Having to live a life with AIDS never got easier each day.

That old Alyssa was certainly all gone now
And may never return again
Not able to be herself no this time she was
Better now than back then.

You can still read about her
And even learn from her too
No matter the situation you go through
God is always there to see you through.

Sometimes we take life for granted
And it's easy to slip up
Even those who don't deserve the pain
Tend to get caught up.

She's All Gone Now but her dream will forever live
In the lives of young men and even women
Get tested and stay protected because AIDS do not discriminate.
Educate yourself as well as your mate.

Then stay connected with God
Through prayer and supplication
Read your Bible everyday
Even if you're on vacation

A Good Thing Gone

I can only imagine the pain you must have felt.
Each time I told you I loved you but with other men I slept.
With and to add insult to injury I got knocked up
Carrying another man's seed in my womb
But yours I aborted.

I'm sorry for not knowing how to love or be loved.
We go way back past the pits that we dug.
I remember the ring you gave me on Valentine's Day.
And if I ever questioned your love for me
It was clear on that day.

The bracelet you gave me for my birthday
Standing in my Pop's kitchen
Had me crying tears of joy
Over a rack of clean dishes

You were everything that I could have ever hoped
For in a man and much more
No other man could have compared
Who could have asked for anything more

I took you for granted and back then I couldn't see
How very much you meant to me
From the movies to dinner, haunted houses and all
The Canal, the long walks, you were there through it all.

From my graduations to child birth, jobs and even moves
I could always count on you; rather I'd win or even lose.
Never being judge mental or telling me how you felt
Struggling with your own hand that was dealt

The Essence Of A Virtuous Woman

Never questioning if the love I had for you was real or not.
But it was and still is you know you have a piece of my heart.
Just understand I had a lot of growing up to do.
I had to finally find me, so I can truly love you.

Despite the joke of a marriage I had to another
You have always been my heart
And not just my lover

You have always been the comparison to men who came after you.
Not competing or coming close, to the love I have for you.
You are the only man my parents and grandparents approved.
Wanted me to marry you long before I would ever say I do

You have always been my friend no matter who was in your life.
When I would call you made it possible,
Didn't matter if it was day or night

You were so in tune with every part of me.
My physical my emotional as well as my sexuality
But I yearned for an intimate connection spiritually.
You would take me to a dimension where I could just escape
I wanted to join hands with you and kneel before God and just pray.

I wanted to read scriptures and elaborate on the Word of God
Between the two of us we could cry out to God
And then rejoice together when we see our prayers that have been answered.

But you seemed to have no interest in knowing God at all
You have been through so much in life
You didn't think that God even cared for you at all.

Even a simple mention of the name of God
You seemed to just shut down
You kept everything bottled up on the inside
Until it seemed like you just didn't even want me around.
Although I never stopped praying for you

I am still praying still to this day.
I need God to show up for you
In a major way

It is my desire to see you saved and set free.
So that you can enjoy life to the fullest
And eternity you can see
I know sometimes life changes so quick
It's like we need a moment to catch up
But there is no way I could enjoy living my life
If there was just a single chance to save your life.

And I neglected to cease it over your lack of understanding
Afraid that I would push you away
Because I was too pushy or demanding
So as I get out of the way and allow God to use me
I will humble myself so my mouth He can use it.

My prayer is that through my testimony you can see God at His best.
You have seen me first hand when I was at my worst,
And yet somehow we are still close today.
And with my faith and hope in God
I know you will be saved.

When it's Time to Boot Up
Men Listen Up

I just want to take the time to talk to the men today.
To give you some advice from a woman's perspective
And show you another way.

We as women no matter if we are black, white, or red.
We want a strong man with a level head.
He has to have ambition and a drive to want to succeed.
But most importantly the love of God
That can be passed down through his seeds.

We would like a man who is strong enough to know
That even he can't fix all things,
But in prayer he should go.

A man who is humble enough to admit when he is wrong
It doesn't make you weak but just proves
You are indeed strong.

A man who is sensitive to a degree
He realizes that God's greatest gift to a man
Is of course his Lady

But a man who will take care of home,
And be responsible for his actions
Rather he is right or wrong.

A man who understands a woman's worth
His objective is to take care of her
At the same time continue encouraging her

Not saying you have to be perfect

But striving to be better
We will have your back through it all
No matter the weather.

We love a man who is eager to supply all of our needs
Catering to our soul in deed
But handling also the fleshes needs.

We don't mind carrying you
When you are too weak from the fight
But you have to be worth us booting up to fight.
Because we can be your "Holy Field", when life knocks you down.
We tag team the enemy, so we can go twelve rounds.

Because while you were fighting for us meaning family and all
We have called on back up
Who has come to settle it all
Because when we fight we don't fight fair,
We call on our Father, The Son and the Holy Spirit.
So we can't fail

We encourage you to communicate
Cause the fight has already been fixed.
But when we touch and agree the enemy can't use his tricks.

To separate what God has ordained.
Our relationship is covered in the blood and
Victory we will proclaim.

So keep your hands to yourself and let God fight for you.
Spend your time putting on the armor of God
And allow Him to guide you.

So men I'm begging you to take heed.
God makes no mistakes
You can be the head of your household
But let God be the head of your life.

He Can Be Saved

Lil Mike started selling dope at such an early age
Pop's was in and out of jail
And he was filled with so much rage.
Pissed off because his mother was weak
Behind these no good men
She stayed in the streets.

Section 8, food stamps, welfare checks
Full time job but the lights stayed on disconnect.
Notice every time he looked up.
But what could he do
In a house full of women
And still he had school

He was gifted in every sport known to man.
But no funds were ever available for him to attend
Extracurricular activities at school.
So money was on his agenda
So of course he broke all the rules.

He got tired of living without
Why should he and his sisters struggle
He'd plan to take a different route

Now the rage he had in him made him such a dangerous man
Heart was cold as an iceberg
And his neighborhood he ran.
Had all the old schools watching him in amazement
Trying to figure out where all the money in the streets went.

Now his goal was to make it and never look back
In the process he got a few degrees and chose to just stack.
His paper like a real man should

Anxiously awaiting the day he could
Move his family up and out the hood

Now Lil Mike was the man in the streets
Supply and demand had him loosing much sleep.
So he would smoke a few blunts and have him a drink
Cause life was like a chess game
And he was the King.

Life was good until he caught his case.
Had to do a bid upstate.
But even then the respect he had established
Along the way
made prison life for a few years
Bearable to stay.

He and his little sisters
Whom he protected at all cost
And at all times and still to this day.
Built such a great relationship
She shared her love for Christ with him one day.

He started to see this change
Take place before his very eyes.
He thought she was high off something
He watched her self-esteem rise.

He made sure she was ok
Didn't matter how much
If she asked he just gave.

Now of course that caused conflict
With the other sisters indeed
Having to deal with all of
The jealousy and envy.

They didn't understand why the bond
Was so strong that they shared.
Not realizing that the abuse as children

The Essence Of A Virtuous Woman

Was the common bond they that shared.

They stayed on punishment so outside they didn't see
He taught her how to play chess
And helped her learn her Japanese.

As they grew older and survived the trials
They both married and had children
And between the two were only miles.

Despite everything they had gone through as kids
Only motivated them to do it big
He's giving his life to
Christ and each day he prays some more
Asking God to keep him
And continue to open up other doors.

His sister OmUnicque is a doctor and evangelist too
He's extremely proud of all she has grown to do.
Then there is Pamela who graduated from Yale University
She is now practicing Law for those plagued by poverty.

And of course there is Mesha who has had it a little hard.
She has been a Professional student at TSU for 8 years
And still has no degree.

Her major changes with each man that she sees.
And of course falls in love with
That girl could have been a doctor by now but no
She is afraid of life after college so,
Lil Mike keeps her tuition paid in full.
But if it made his sisters happy he would certainly play the fool.
If Pops was still alive He would be proud too
Because his children have set out to do
Just what God has called them to do.

Lil Mike has a multi-million dollar business
Empowering young men across the globe.
Rather they are in jail or free

His main goal in life is to teach.

And reach those men who may have lost all hope.
Serving time in prisons for selling dope
These are men who have a mindset for business
Some of them are even wonderful chemists.

He focuses on their strengths and then teaches them to play
The game of life from a winning perspective.
Through biblical teachings and practical terms
These men startup businesses and firms.

Playing with the stock market
Investments and such,
CD's IRA's Savings Bonds and of course
Money for a rainy day.

He teaches them how to become wealthy
in every aspect of their lives.
By applying the biblical teachings
They can truly enjoy life.

So even though Lil Mike was the man in the streets
His testimony will be able to reach
Souls that the enemy wants
To sift as wheat.
But the battle the enemy has already lost
So I say this to encourage some hearts
God will meet you at the point of your need
Even if you feel lost.
So don't let your situation keep you from knowing
Christ
Just invite him to be a part of your personal life.

Fed Up

Now I know I'm not crazy, I don't drink or smoke weed.
So please explain to me
Who gave him permission to hit me?

Last time I checked I was grown
With kids of my own.
So clearly this Negro has lost his mind
It has to be completely gone.

How did we get here?
Did I miss a turn somewhere?
We used to be so in love,
Had lots in common and
Smiles we would share.

It seems like one day he came home a changed man.
Clearly not the man I fell in love with.
Naw, this one here I can't stand.

I used to be his favorite person in the whole wide world.
Now it's like I don't know him.
Heck I don't even care.

Seems like he went from complimenting my shape,
To punching me in my side, then even that escalated to rape.

It used to be the only time he would grab a hold to my hair,
Was in the bedroom being intimate exchanging lustful stares

He used to kiss me on my neck, and tell me honey I'm home.
Now it's like I watch the clock, praying that he won't return home.
What changed between then and now?
Seems like nothing I do can erase that frown.

It's like he's always upset and mad because he is here.
Although nothing is stopping him from leaving
But the fear is what keeps him here.

We argue more than we talk no more sweet whispers
It's only screaming and hollering
Name calling, hitting and kicking

My hair is tattered and my cheeks are stained from my tears.
It's like as each one leaves my face I lose a bit more fear.

Between the black and blue bruises some old and some fresh
Thinking one day this man will kill me
If I stay in this mess.

No one to talk too, way too afraid of what people might say.
I can hear the ridicule in their voices now as they would say
"Hmm umm that's what she gets,
For marrying that man and so quick"

"She thought she was all that because she got herself a husband".
Not knowing that he was crazy as hell on the other hand,
Not having the courage to speak up.
Cause if my family knew what I had endured they would
All be locked up.

But because I had a battle with my self esteem
Not realizing that I too was a queen.
But instead I'm reduced to being a punching bag
Every single time this crazy fool gets mad.

So what do I do?
I have children who need me too.
I used to think that I was sexy,
But now I'm not so sure.
Seems like the only thing people see
When they look at me
Are the cuts and bruises, maybe even the sores

The Essence Of A Virtuous Woman

My stress level seems to have risen,
To a level I can't seem to control.
I couldn't tell you if I was coming or going
And now my attitude is so cold.

I feel the hatred boiling inside of me,
Knowing this is not what God has intended for me.
Certainly if I stay I will be destined for hell.
Or writing letters to my family from the inside
Of a jail cell.

But either case there has to be a better way.
To escape this hell of a marriage
And start a brand new day.

I know for a fact he has one more time
To slap me, punch me, choke or push me.
Before I lose the sense God gave me
And just shoot him.

I'm fed up and a victim I will no longer be.
I'm through playing house and allowing him to beat me.
Somebody should have told him
That I was at my wits end
Now I'm sitting here looking at blood shed
Repenting for my sins

Not really sure who's blood I see.
Cause all I can remember is darkness
Heck I thought I was still sleep.

When I opened my eyes I could see me.
With an iron skillet in my hand
And his body is laid out at my feet

I hear crying but I'm not sure it's my voice
Maybe it's the kids I just knew I had no choice.
It's either him or me and I know I've done nothing wrong.
Besides loving this man with all of me

And suffering for far too long

He's not moving and I can't tell if he's breathing
I don't think I even care
Because it all started over chicken.

I made pork chops and gravy for dinner
With mashed potatoes and green beans
After 3am he comes in throwing things.

Had the nerve to pull me out of my bed
After I told him he should have stayed gone
That's when my head.
Hit the hardwood floor, and I felt the baby ball up.
Didn't matter that I was carrying his child
I felt like I had simply had enough.

He drug me kicking and screaming into the kitchen.
I was praying all the while, I was hoping and wishing.
That just maybe, he would come to his senses.

And realize that it's not me who causes him this pain.
But I'm the one he claims, he loves
Although this relationship has gotten insane.

Always threatening to leave
But that's a promise he never kept.
I had been praying that he would just leave
Before it would have ever come to this.

I can see me hitting him uncontrollably,
until his scull cracked open.
Am I wrong for wanting him dead,
Because I was praying, I was hoping.

I hear a man screaming police
and banging on the door with a stick
Now I'm thinking to myself
Where did they come from and so quick?

It seems like when the tables were turned
the police would take all day
Now all of sudden they at my door
Ready to take me away.

But I will be darned if I let you lock me up
When it's this sucka who has lost his mind
And it's me who's had enough.

I don't need IMPD standing looking at me
Like I'm the one in the wrong
For not letting him beat me.

Oh but she want to get smart
And look at me like I'm nothing.
I don't care if you are the police
That ain't gone stop me from cussing.

That's right get his weak a** up outta here.
Now you can fill in the blank.
Cause I'm tired of this physco joker
Messing up my face.

This selfish egotistical poor pitiful excuse for a man
I hope he dies before he can reach
The back of an ambulance

I hear her telling me to calm down
But chick where were you at,
When he was dragging me across this ground?

She told me if I kept getting smart she would lock me up.
I told her to take her insensitive tale out my door
Cause clearly I didn't give a f***.

Please excuse my language, while the picture I paint clearly
Because that day I can say
I was truly lucky.

With each blow I struck
That power I gained back.
He was more shocked at the fact
I had enough strength to fight back.

I used to be so weak and would endure whatever he had.
No matter the words that escaped his lips
With the intention to make me sad,

But with each insult and bruise I thought about
Just pissed me off more
Made me mad at myself for continuing to endure.

Life and death is in the power of your own tongue.
His words hurt more than the actual blows.
Because those he shot from his mouth
Targeted at my self esteem
Believing his hurtful lies that were so mean.

Not having the spirit of God to counter act his behavior.
Needing the Lord to show up and be more than just my savior.
But the thing is God has always been there.
Giving me a choice to life when death was in the air.

I chose to continue to stay with a man, who only knew pain,
A culture that kept him in bondage and chains.
So if I'm talking to you then set free you can be
By choosing life through Christ
You will be able to finally see.

Real love and not the love that's fraudulent
All you have to do is Repent.
Ask God to help you and protect you as well
Then keep you in perfect peace.

It's those times that you are really going through
When God is present and carrying you
It's He that kept breathing life into me.

Telling me how much He Himself loves me.

And that His grace and mercy is sufficient enough
And through him I can choose life.
Even when times get tough
So even though abuse we know all too well
God has another chance to show you
He can protect you from hell

So be encouraged and blessed just the same
God loves you and He cares
Just listen He is calling your name.

Bridgette N. Thornton

I Love Me Enough

I love me enough to look at the ringing phone.
When I know it's you on the other end
Not wanting to be alone.

I love me enough to say no
When you want to touch me, in places
That should be touched only by my husband.

I love me enough to turn a deaf ear.
When you want to whisper to my flesh
With words I don't need to hear.

I love me enough to set the example for my babies,
On how we are to behave has women of God while
We are waiting.

When it comes to sex God loves us so much
That he has set aside his very best.
I love me enough to say no more abuse
Not physical, not mental, or even sexual.

I love me enough to embrace every aspect of me.
Every pound and strand of hair, my smile heck, even my teeth.
I love me enough to respect myself and no longer allowing myself
To settle for less.

I love me enough to wait
On the man God created for me
I know it's not too late.

I love me enough to fight for my soul
When the enemy comes in like a flood
I can be bold or so I'm told.

I love me enough to raise the bar
High enough you would have to duck to

Keep from hitting the stars.

I love me enough to really take care of me
While I'm waiting I will preserve
All that is me.

I love me enough to love me
And depend on God to really show me.

What loving me is all about.
So I read my word and meditate daily and I watch
What comes out of my mouth.

I love me enough to speak life to you as well
For I am a reflection of my Father
And the good news I will tell.

So in loving me enough I have to love you too.
For God so loved the world He gave His only begotten
Son For me as well as for you.

Bridgette N. Thornton

Ok So I Date

Who said I can't love and keep my faith?
Nowhere in the Bible does it say I can't date
Especially when God is love and we have been taught to hate.

So why do women get condemned for wanting a little romance?
Every man we date will most likely
Not be our husband.

Being a woman of God my priorities should not change because I date.
My main goal in life is to serve God
And allow Him to choose my mate.

Now the Bible says to acknowledge God in all of my ways.
So I simply give Him honor in all I do
And praise Him each and every day.

Now to be a lady of the Lord I must carry myself as such
Dinner and a movie maybe even a light lunch.
Just because I'm dating doesn't mean I'm having sex.
If he's a man of God then he will respect my wishes.

And if he is the man for me
Then he would be attending church
On Sunday and in attendance for Bible study.

And because we are dating then of course we should line up.
With the Word of God because in Him we both trust.
Not to mention being a light in the darkness of others
By simply taking the time to share my testimony.

Now I'm not saying that we pretend to be perfect because we're not
I'm just saying that even in dating
God should mean a lot.

To the both of us and compromising His time is not an option
We have to continue to pray, and read our Word and
Continue to seek His instructions.

There has to be some principals, morals and values of course.
Even though we've made mistakes it's important to stay the course
God has no respect of persons
And He will give you your hearts desires.
But it's in acknowledging Him and all that you do.
And not being a liar.

Because you can front and play church if that's what you choose to do.
But He sees all and He knows all so be careful
With what you do.
Especially how you treat people,
Cause in the presence of God you will be.
So even in an intimate relationship
The God within you should be clear to see.

So what if I'm dating because you just never know
It's possible I'm entertaining my husband
But only God really knows.

Bridgette N. Thornton

How Do You Love Without First Loving Self?

How do you truly love someone, without first loving self?
You go through the motions
Until there is nothing left.

You spend countless hours trying to figure out why
Everyone around you is giving love a try.
When you look in the mirror your reflection is quick to say
No man will ever love you
No not today.

Those seeds have been planted in your spirit, way back when.
And now you're old enough to experience it but then.
Here come those thoughts that paralyze your dream
Your dream of being loved and now it seems.

That each relationship you enter is sabotaged from the start.
Not knowing if he loves you for real
Truly with all of his heart.

Having the opportunity to be loved past the pain.
Has never presented itself so clearly
There is simply nothing at all to gain.

So you search and you search but instead you're introduced to lust.
Because it feels so good momentarily
You felt that you had to rush.

Just in case he realizes that you are not the one.
Then maybe there is another and clearly he is done.
But in all actuality the love for you he has had plenty.
But because you didn't love yourself
Your heart has been left empty.

You start to lose your self-worth, and self-esteem is gone too.

You settle for less in search of someone to love you.
You settle for being mistreated
And neglected to say the least
You end up pregnant by a bunch of dead beats.

And then you wonder have I ever really truly been loved?
You find that one who stuck around through it all.
Waiting patiently for you to find your way
Through your darkest of days just so he can say.
"I have always loved you even before you were born
To your mother
Before God spoke you into existence I have never loved another".

"I have always loved you, even when you were unable to see.
The love I have for you, buried deep within me.
I have always loved you, every part that makes you who you are.
From every freckle, every mole, every hair, every scar".

"I have always loved you enough to go to God and pray.
That if it be His will then you would love me just the same.
I have always loved you even in the midst of my own storm.
I love you enough to be patient, and wait for you to come home".

"I have always loved you because you are a part of me
Flesh of my flesh, bone of my bone.
Because the blood of Christ was shed for you and me".

"My love for you is not from what the natural eye can see.
It's not your walk or your talk or your shape that's so sexy.
It's not because of the car you drive, or the home you reside in
I love you because God made me just like Him".

"And in obedience I will keep the vow to love you
As Christ loves the Church and even if you can't love you.
The love I will show you can only draw you near.
And through prayer and supplication you will be able to hear".

"God confirming the love I have for you and then we will see.
How very capable you are of loving me".

So again I ask how do you truly love someone without first loving self?
You fall in love with the one, who made you,
Who sacrificed Himself

And then you ask Him to teach you how to love
How to submit and respect and to discern
And then to be obedient and open to learn.

Then forgive yourself and those who intentionally planted the seeds.
That said you couldn't be loved past all of your needs.

And then you listen to the Holy Spirit because He is there to guide you.
He will place you right in the heart of the one
Who He created to truly love you

Sweet Dreams

I see visions of you playing my body like a slow groove.
Melodic ecstasy touching me, while I'm touching you.
It's like that old school, that groove
So sensual and so smooth.

Not bumping and grinding but a slow walk
Hand in hand I hear you whisper and not talk
But we unwind, as we pass time
As you remove all garments in slow motion,
We press rewind
Wanting to savor every moment in time.

It's like I imagine each kiss strategically placed from on lips
And from my lips to my hips you watch me strip
As I look into your eyes I can tell you are so loving it.
So I don't trip.

As your hands rub and feel every aspect of my flesh
I'm reminded of the love depicted in the book of Solomon that was expressed.
When she said," how handsome you are my beloved, Oh how charming", She had to be talking about you
Because as each moment passes I find myself thinking of you

Thinking of the rhythm that sways from the passion as you explore
The very essence of my nectar that seeps through
My G-string from that special door

Or should I say gateway to the sheer existence of sweet romance that tingles with each touch
Waiting in agony drives me crazy with the simplest touch. But you don't rush

You take your time just like I like because the wait has its advantages
You're making love to my mind and not my flesh I can't stand it

So as the Isley Brothers play in the back of my mind
I'm reminded of the words that say "we are two hearts on Fire that have been ignited
So just know I want you longer than for one night
We are united.

I want your heart for a lifetime
I want the promises my grandparents had
I want the pleasures the pains and all that is you
I want you to need me as I desire you

As I arch my back to receive the love that you have been waiting to sample
I'm like an all you can eat buffet, but can you handle it?
The simplicity of me who only desires to be
That special lady in your life I'll be she and you'll be he.

We would make love continuously
While listening to Ron Isley sing between the sheets
Because that's exactly where I want to be

I want to straddle and mount the delectable manhood that's past erection
It's eagerly awaiting the warmness and the wetness
My breast caramel complected
I slide down, slowly and gracefully I take my time

I rock and grind as I roll my hips
You see my eyes roll in the back of my head as I kiss your lips

I feel your hands gripping my rear
Listening to your sweet moans in my ear
I loose myself with each thrust causing my legs to shake while you moan my name
I can barely take it, the sweat dripping down from my face

But you getting it in Ummmm and I'm loving it
It's seems as though the minutes have turned into hours

The Essence Of A Virtuous Woman

The time is flying and I'm trying
To make you come in and on places that you can't even imagine.
Then I tell you exactly what you're thinking and of course we both laugh
Because I know you want to bend me over so my hair you can grab it.
So I oblige, I bend over and I put it in the air
Feeling you enter me from behind so our love we can continue to share.

I feel me cumming Daddy don't stop is what I say.
Biting down on the pillows so you can have your way.
I tell you get it Daddy and that's all you need to hear
It's like that open invitation to release
You grab my hair.

And as we let go it's so amazing because we explode in unison
But far from done, this is only part one
Then I awake and realize I'm alone
And immediately I reach for my cell phone.

I dial your number so your voice I can hear and listen to you tell me you miss me and can't wait to get here.
So I put it on pause and patiently I wait
For you my husband, my friend, my lover and soul mate.
Because the bed of marriage is undefiled at least that's what the word says.
Because He who finds a wife finds a good thing,
So my husband can clearly relate.

He is stationed in Fort Worth Texas and is due to deploy soon,
Sometimes I hate that he enlisted in the Army
But he has to do what he has been called to do.

Yes it is to protect and serve our nation
But being a military wife gets hard when you have been left to raise a baby.
Although don't get me wrong I support him to the end.
But my bed gets cold at night especially while missing my man.

He has left so many memories of his love making ability
My body seems to crave for him the longer he is away from me.
He knows how to keep me busy while staying on his mind
Between the nasty little text messages and our personal face time.

I am proud of my man especially when he wears his uniform.
So sexy and strong I just can't wait for him to come home.
Our daughter is 7 months
And she has only seen her Father once.

I replay over and over again the night she was conceived.
You were home on a pass to burry your Dad.
Going through a lot of emotional pain
Not able to say your last good byes
For being overseas almost drove you insane.

I remember holding you in my arms while the tears escaped your eyes.
I held you so close while I wiped the tears from your eyes.
We cried together because your father meant a lot
To the both of us and now the suffering has stopped.
You still can't help but grieve in your own way
Full of frustration and tension because home you couldn't stay.

You knew after all that has happened, you would still have to leave
Me at home for who knows how long and in deed you would miss me.
After crying and holding one another after the family was gone.
I ran a hot bubble bath so you could unwind from it all.

You sat down and pulled me near.
Planted sweet kisses on my face and my ears.
You thanked me for making all of the arrangements on your behalf.
And expressed how appreciative you were and then laughed.

You couldn't believe how sexy I was looking to you
And realized at that moment you wanted to make love to me too.

The Essence Of A Virtuous Woman

So of course anything to please my wonderful husband
I slowly undressed and stepped inside the bath tub.

Almost immediately my Mandingo rose to attention
And so I took the seat upon my thrown
Because we both know I'm the queen in this castle so
I did that little thing that drives you bananas
I did the sit and squeeze as I rode you backwards.

We continued to share each other in the bath tub
Filled with the two of us
In the midst of shear ecstasy Oh' my I have missed you so much.
You don't rush.
But in fact you take your time. As if you were trapped inside of me
Searching for a way to escape you go deep.

I hear you moaning and crying all at the same time
Mixed emotions leave a trail of you in my insides.
You have made love to my soul like never before
We experienced love making from a spiritual point

But when you climaxed in my walls I knew our baby was formed
Because she was conceived in love and during a period
When you were going through the storm

But with each memory, each dream and every time
I look in our daughters face.
I'm reminded of the love we share and the beautiful
Love that we make.

So with each sweet dream
You will continue to be the star
As I press rewind each time no matter how far.

Bridgette N. Thornton

Get Low

What the devil meant for bad,
God will turn it around for your good.
The same thing you were faithful with,
God will get the glory as He should.

Prime example, Tonya was known in the streets.
By the real freaky things she did with her tongue in the sheets.
Now let's just say with sex Tonya was no stranger.
Realizing with each partner
She put herself in more danger.

She was known by her trade mark
Which was getting low
No matter where or when
She had to get that dough.

But what people didn't understand
Was the reason behind it all.
You see Tonya was a product of her environment
She had no one to call.

Suffering from depression,
She had enough sense to pray.
To pray for protection and a way out
For her and her son and of course
A place for them to stay.

Tonya got pregnant at the age of twelve,
Mom was strung out on cocaine and they say
She couldn't provide a place for them to stay.
So she dropped out in elementary school
Determined to love her baby she would
Do what she had to do.

She knew there was a God because a friend of hers went to church.

The Essence Of A Virtuous Woman

She would tell Tonya all the time
It's gone be alright just pray.
Melissa was only thirteen at the time
But she taught Tonya how to pray and
Trusted God would change her mind.

Melissa continued to teach Tonya every chance that she would get.
Instead of just school work she shared scriptures
Along with it.
Melissa never judged her but spoke nothing but the Word.
She spoke life into the situation
Of her closest friend.

She understood that Tonya had to take care of her baby.
So Melissa's first job was babysitting.
She changed diapers, fixed bottles
And even sang to the baby, while Tonya
Was off getting low Melissa prayed for her and the baby.

Tonya would come in after she was done for the night.
Take a long bath to wash away the sins of men
And pray that God would make things right.

She thanked Him for her protection while she was still in her sin.
And for His grace and mercy, and for bringing her back in.
She asked Him to be her provider
Because she was so lost
She got tired of being teased and talked about.

People didn't' understand that her education was slim to none,
Since she got pregnant with her mother's boyfriends son.
She was never quite the same, but she knew there had to be a God
for real.
Because even in the midst of it all, it's like she would just be still.

And just sit in silence and wait for him to speak.
However the only thing she could hear was a voice telling her to
SEEK.
Every now and then she would hear GET LOW.

But how could that be when she was labeled the neighborhood hoe.

After a few years had passed Melissa never stopped praying
And continued to watch Tonya's baby.
This one particular night is one they would never forget.
Tonya was crying and praying trying not to trip.
That very same voice she heard crystal clear this time.
Telling her to GET LOW, but it was different this time.

He told her that her prayers had been answered when she first prayed.
Her sins had been forgiving and He had provided a place
For her to stay

But under two conditions,
She had to share her story
To anyone who would listen.
Then she had to continue to GET LOW
And that's where she would hear instructions
And the story to be told.

As she got low her head was on the floor
And it was there she noticed a small crack in the floor.
After lifting up the tiles, before her very eyes she saw,
Stacks and stacks of cash,
She wasn't sure where it had come from
Maybe it's someone's stash.

As she cried and cried Melissa came to see what was wrong.
She saw all of the money and she began to sing this song.
Get Low, Get Low, Get Low Get Low.
As God told her for every tear shed He gave her double.
For every prayer Melissa prayed she got triple.

Still not understanding how it all happened,
God explained that her Mom had known all along
And that she had been praying for a raven.
To come feed her just in case she would be
Too far gone

And because he called her for a time as this,
To forgive her of all of her wrongs.

She had enough money to supply all her needs.
She stopped sleeping with men for money
But instead she talked to teens.

She paid her tithes and shared her testimony.
To young girls in the hood having sex for money
She explained that even to this day.
God is still providing.
He met her at her lowest point,
And all she had to do is try him.

Her friend Melissa has her own business now.
She runs a safe haven for the children of moms who
Still choose to Get Down.

And just like she prayed for Tonya she is still praying today.
For all the other mothers to eventually find their way.
Back to God where there is safety in His arms.
Where they can be free from sin, and away from all harm

God has blessed her triple fold
For being obedient and doing as she was told
The two are still the best of friends today.
They both continue to Get Low, so
They can hear the voice of God
And to touch and agree as they pray.

Bridgette N. Thornton

Thinking Back

I can smell the urine from the hallways that reek
Each time I open my door.
From the boys who claim to be men
Yet they piss all over the floor.

Can't go outside to play, there were no fenced in backyards.
Only dimly lit hallway corridors
Where the older cats sat and played cards.

No air conditioners on the hot summer days.
Only an open window with a box fan
Rotating as the nights turn into days.

No steaks and baked potatoes
Or salad when we sat
down at night for dinner.
How about bologna sandwiches, sugar bread
And peanut butter spread over celery sticks
Now that was a winner.

If you lay quietly enough you could hear the big wheels
Go flying down the hallway.
In a concrete jungle where there
Was no room for little kids to play.

Eating koolie cups to keep cool, there were no trees to provide shade.
Only cracked sidewalks and pot holes
Police tape and white chalk,
Outlining where dead bodies once lay.

There were no nannies or babysitting,
If you were the oldest you had the job.
Never mind if you were old enough
You held it down when mom was gone.

The Essence Of A Virtuous Woman

You were taught at an early age to be thankful for what you got.
To take pride in yourself even if you didn't have a lot.
Not used to Daddy's being in the picture
No not at all
So the strong black woman is the role model
That you saw.

Working two jobs that pay next to nothing
Because the welfare she didn't want
To prideful to take hand me downs
So she made the clothes her children wore.

She would work extra hours just to
Provide a Sunday dinner worth eating.
Establishing a tradition that one day
Her children would stick with.

However the most important thing that was taught
If nothing else.
Is that prayer changes all things
And not to expect nothing less.

Education is so important
Cause it paints that foundation of who
You would grow to be.
This is why you go to school and do the best
That you can do.
Be whoever God called you to be.

So I said this to say it's not how you began
But what it's all about is
The lives you change in the end

We all have a story to tell
And we need ears to hear
Lives to change each and every day
By sharing our testimony

Exceptional men and women

Have been birthed right out of the hood
While society was looking down on them
They were able to still see the good.

It takes a little faith
Some hope and a vision maybe a dream
To take a simple situation that seems
Like there will never be a chance to elevate.
Beyond normal or maybe even right
While trying to set a foundation for children
Those who come after you in life.

We have to have a sense of pride
And enough sense to give back
By living our lives as examples and help those
Who seem to lack.

Because rather you reside in the White House
Or the trailer parks down the street.
God can use the least of us
To save those He has to reach

We all have a responsibility to remain humble
While being blessed.
Because despite where we come from
God still expects our best.

The problem as I see it each and every day
People getting the big head,
Living outside of God's will
Not caring what they say.

Some seem to think that degree's and titles are a must.
But if God isn't getting the glory
Then it all becomes just stuff.

We have all been called to disciple
And share the good news about Jesus Christ.
And in doing so you go through some things

The Essence Of A Virtuous Woman

To prepare you for this life.

Your past sets the foundation of a testimony to give.
Things you have overcome trials and even where you lived.

It's not about the past or the tests along the way
But rather or not God is at the head of your life
Getting the glory in each and every way.

Different stages for Him to have the lead role.
To share with the unbelievers
He is concerned about their souls.

So in the midst of being blessed stay connected to God and see
How even through all your mess
Humility is always the best.

Thinking back is always a good reminder of how far you have come along
Just don't stay there for too long
Continue to look forward and expect something great
Allow God to shape your future
Because your life is at stake.
The enemy comes to steal kill and destroy.
He wants to sift us as wheat
By using our past against us
Since he has no control over our future.

But by being in Christ and knowing God as our keeper
The enemy has no dominion over us
Because we are truly God's people.

So in thinking back continue to see the light
The salvation of our Lord and Savior
Jesus Christ.

Bridgette N. Thornton

My Mother

My mother is such an exceptional mother
Words could hardly explain,
How much she has tried to be a good mother
Through the sunshine and the rain.

Now I'm not saying she is perfect
Because flaws we all conceal.
But one thing I know for sure
And that is she's my only mother for real.

I guess you can say we grew up together.
along the way we had trials and errors.
I think she was a free spirit trying to find her own place in this world
.Back then it was normal to have a baby as a young girl.
.

I used to blame her for everything wrong in my life
Instead of accepting responsibility for my own actions
And doing what I knew to be right.

I can say she put up with some hell from me.
But it was only because she didn't know me
I had fears from experiences that no little girl should know.

So I blamed her because as a mother, I felt she should have just known
I was constantly crying out for help
In my attitude as well as my actions
I wanted to be loved and held and to give her some satisfaction.

I needed her to be proud of me
To hug me and simply say she loves me.
If a little affection and time could cure all the pain
Then I would go back to the day it all began.

The Essence Of A Virtuous Woman

And just erase every bad moment away
Then replace it with walks, bare feet in the grass as I play.
I would tell my mother each and everyday
That God loves her in such a special way.

I would comfort her instead of bringing her a beer.
Because of the abuse she suffered
Kept us all in fear.
But there would be no more tears.
I would rub her feet after working all day
I would encourage her with words of endearment as I would say
Mommy can we please pray?

I would make pictures for her to get lost in.
To imagine a life where we wouldn't have to wonder when.
But we'd know how God is indeed our provider
So she wouldn't have to hang out with the Motor Cycle Riders,

In the presence of my Mother, she would just know
That no matter what happened God is setting her
Up for an over flow.

An abundance of peace, joy and everything else
Because she gave birth to a King and Queens
So she'll have plenty of wealth.

I would tell my Mother what an amazing
Sense of humor she had.
And I would do anything in my power
To keep her from being mad or ever being sad

I would tell her she was gorgeous,
Even flawless you see.
A direct reflection of God our Creator
Who said in Psalms 139:14
That she is fearfully and wonderfully made
And I'm glad she looks a lot like me.

Because my Mother is a lot like

Other mothers you will meet
She did what she had to do
In order for her children to eat

So instead of complaining I've learned to encourage
Now as an adult I tend to change the role.
I make sure my Mommy is straight.
I pray for her deliverance and that
God guides her in all her ways.

That He orders her steps
So she can clearly see.
That God has a wonderful plan for her
As well as for me.

So with that being said my mommy, I only have one
She cannot be replaced by another one.

I love her and stand to bridge the gap.
I pray and intercede because I got her spiritual back.
She answers to B-Rocka, B- Dubb or just plain Bridgette Wallace
if you call her by her name
However I get the pleasure of calling her Mom, Ma, Mother, and Mommy
And my favorite My Suga Mommy
And that name can never ever be changed

Senior Dream Team

Some say you all are seasoned seniors,
But I say you all are pillars full of wisdom.
Some say yes they are indeed wise.
But I see love and faith when I look into your eyes.

Some say your rich,
From all the suffering you've endured.
But I say I'm grateful,
For all of the love that has been poured.

Out and into the lives of not just myself,
But into my children as well
For the generations of wisdom,
And advice that you love to share

Some may have called you old
And even past your prime.
I say thank you Lord for the sacrifices
That have been made over time.

To help pave the way for a soul like mine.
Who is ready, willing, and able, to accept the baton.
In this race we call life
To make it easier for those who come behind me.
I want to share in the love and joy and to make others happy.

Some say the elders in the church should always pray
But I say thank you for teaching me
How to be faithful through prayer

I thank you for setting the example
For women such as me
Continually serving God our Father
Through your actions, make it easier for me.

Some say you all are church members

But I have to disagree,
Because to my family and I
You all are a part of my family

I carry you all in my spirit
And on the top of my prayer list
Is where each member of this Senior Dream Team sits
I look forward to our mid-week services
Just to fellowship with you.
Because I know you all
Have been praying for me too
I see your smiles and I feel your hugs
With each kiss on my cheek
Let's me know I'm truly loved.

So in case no one has told you
Or at least not today
I love you all so much
And in every way

You all make being away from home
Such a breeze
My mom doesn't have to even
Worry about me
Because even she knows I'm in good hands.
God has placed me amongst some angels
And through your prayers I can continue to stand.

Surrender

It's so crazy because so many people have watched her in shear amazement.
With this attitude and poise about her no matter the circumstances.
She always managed to keep a beautiful smile on her face.
You only knew what she was going through when she allowed you in her space.

Some people had no idea of the battle she was fighting.
When her household was sleep she managed to be praying.
She would intercede on behalf of those who didn't know Christ.
She had no respect of persons didn't matter if they were black or white.

She knew that she had a responsibility to go to God in prayer and even fast at times
In spite of all her trials she managed to stay close to Christ during difficult times.
She was just one of those people who really didn't meet any strangers at all.
She had an obligation to share her love for God with each one of us all.

She went from being this awesome woman, exceptional parent, and beautiful friend.
To not knowing if on her own two legs she would be able to stand.
She went from income to take care of her house and maybe a few more also.
To not knowing if God was angry at her cause inside she felt awful.

How could she minister effectively to the hearts and minds of God's people?
When she was learning how to trust all over again, it was like a never ending sequel.
Not to mention she had the weight of the world on her shoulders

Trying to keep a positive attitude and live off of God's promises.

She speaks life to her situation and has faith that it will change
However her flesh will sometimes get in the way
Being so far from home she knows that failure is not an option.
Although she gets lonely however her salvation she won't compromise with.

She knows that she has been called to be the salt of the earth.
The light on hill if you will chose by God to lead his people since birth.
She has an awesome task on her hands yearning to do her best
Knowing she has been called and set apart from all of the rest

So trusting God is in her DNA for sure
However she still has that fleshly part of man that makes
It hard for her to soar

So to watch her from a distance is like watching a gazelle.
She exemplifies the beauty of God in the earth realm
A virtuous woman in all her splendor with a heck of a story to tell

Overcoming the whiles of the enemy from birth he thought he had her trapped.
Said she would be nothing as a matter of fact.
So many people have believed that lie as it was told.
Over the years she has proven that the love of God still flows.

Being torn between good and bad, right and wrong or even up and down was an everyday thing for Unicque.
Seemed like as each day went by it got harder and harder for her to think

She was a faithful member of her church she tried her best to focus on Christ
But with each trial each test had her thinking twice.
Now she didn't smoke but occasionally she had a drink
Especially when life was too much to handle she found it easier for her to think.

She would date here and there but no one in particular caught her eye
Until one day she meets a special kind of guy.
He was intelligent and witty he seemed to have all of the right things to say.
Was a tad bit older but still special in his own way
Now he wasn't the most handsome man she'd ever laid eyes on
But there was something about his boldness that had her so gone.

This man was full of experience and to say the things he did to her had to be a sin.
But in her eyes that was the man for her and God would forgive her in the end.
She thought because she was faithful to him than they would live happily ever after at least that what she thought
True they had their differences but she was a forgiving kind of person even though they rarely fought.

They didn't go out much either cause he was conservative with his money.
She says he is cheap so cheap it wasn't funny.
He was level headed and she liked to shop.
While he planned for their future she would shop until she dropped.

They never really saw eye to eye but he had his ways of compromising.
She fell for him each time and somehow she'd end up crying.
Determined to make it work and not be alone.
She just accepted all that he was rather it was right or even wrong.
She longed for him to pray with her and even go to church
He was scorned before by the church folk and vowed never to step foot into another church.

He knew God for himself although Jesus was not his Savior.
There was nothing that Unicque could say,
In order to make him a believer

She prayed and prayed that he would change so that they could live as one
Although he acknowledged God, but shows no reverence for His Son

Now she was torn because if he knew Jesus in the way she's known Him for a while
He would be able to bridge the gap as the head of their household

He would have the power to change situations by speaking the Word.
And since Jesus is the way the truth and the life, then through Christ
He'd be free as a bird.

Then he would be able to experience healing and deliverance
From all of his pain and all of his afflictions
But even more important they could pray together
They could touch and agree.
With the two of them together praying the enemy will have to flee.
But because they are not in agreement
The enemy has a legal right to be.
Present and wreaking havoc
Making it harder for Unique

Because although she is in love and believes that God will save him
That doesn't stop the attacks from coming.
They only come more frequently.
So she begins to think,
"Is this relationship actually worth all the pain I have to suffer"?
Or should I just throw in the towel but that doesn't stop me from loving him".

She's thinking "the harder she prays the worst it all gets
Could this be a sign that she shouldn't deal with it?
But then what if his salvation is attached to her faithfulness?
And what if she is the reason God brought her to him"?

All these things run through her mind.
It's like Lord say something because she doesn't want to waste her time.
She understands that Salvation is a choice.
But what happens if she walks away and for some reason he perishes.

Why would God allow her to fall in love with a man?
Even though we were born sinners.
What exactly is the plan?
All things work together for the good of them who love the Lord
And are called according to His purpose
But how can she know for sure she is making the right decision?

It's hard to stay saved when you are going through hell and.
Is it because she is living in sin
Or from God's grace has she fallen?

Unicque couldn't understand it nothing seemed to be making any sense.
How could God allow her to be so deeply in love with a man who doesn't love Jesus?
So how is she supposed to marry this man?
When the word says that love covers a multitude of sin
And to love one another as Christ loves the church,
It's a million and one scriptures that depict God's love for us and the earth.

So it became very clear to her as if the light bulb was turned on.
Surrender it all to God and let Him draw him home.
She was only supposed to lead him to the water.
It wasn't her job to make him drink.
God said to draw near to Him and he would draw him to thee.

She just had to continue to live her life and walk in her calling
And when her boyfriend hears his call
Then he would come running.
Everybody will not get saved the exact same way.
Some people may not hear God when He calls there name.

But if you stay in prayer and stay connected to God
He will in deed give you your hearts desire
You can truly have it all.

If Jesus wrote you a letter in response
To a prayer that you prayed

Hey there,
I'm writing you on behalf of the woman that
You prayed for to be
Your wife
I'm excited to let you know that she needs a man like you in her life.

She also understands that you come baring gifts,
A total package if you will a bundle of beautiful children
So remarkable but yet still.

Your life is incomplete, like a void that should be filled.
With the love, compassion and prayer of a woman
That's been sealed.

By the Holy Ghost and trying to fulfill
The promises that were made to her by God when He said
"I will never hold any good thing from you", so she is lead
To a strong black man with confidence and poise
A grown man at his finest
Leaving the toys for the little boys

Every conversation is like another page of a good book.
She finds herself waiting for the phone to ring
She checks to make sure it's not off the hook.

In deed a virtuous woman who fears God.
Walks by His Word and in Him she trusts with her all.
So I say this to say, if the opportunity presents itself and it will.
She would like to get to know you and feel.
Apart of every aspect that is you
She believes that God is incapable of making a mistake
So there is no question of why she met you.
Just know that God loves her and has created her to love you.

Now only you will determine how deep her love will flow through you.
She's willing to take the chance and see just how deep your love will flow.
By extending her love to you first, opens the door for you to show.

To show her what it's like to be loved by a real man
What it's like to be admired, adored, and prayed for.

So I will share a few tips on how to make it all work for you.
Simply go to God in prayer and ask Him for permission to date her
And in turn watch Him bless you.

Then after that's done find out what she likes
Pray with her and for her and listen out for her dislikes.

Pay close attention because when she speaks you'll find out
How to please her spiritually and intellectually no doubt

And then once you have connected on that level the rest will be a breeze
You will find out sooner than later that she aims to simply please.

Just know that she's a woman of God first, and a Mother to her children second of course.
However at the same time she is all you will ever need, desire, or even want.

She plays for keeps but it's the long haul that she's in for.
Deserving of being loved unconditionally and cared for
She will cover every aspect of loving you.
From the physical to the spiritual, the mental an even the sexual

So if you decide to step out on faith
Get to know her past what you read on her page.

Spend some time with her and her family
Whichever one is best

And watch how God is faithful and true.
You both will be immensely blessed.

HOOD LOVE

As Majors sat in the driver's seat of her Maserati contemplating her next move.
She replayed the scene over and over again while not really being in the mood.

Terrance from Haughville had once again played her to the left, and for the last time.
She had given him her all for as far back she could remember.
She was his ride or die
Majors was prepared to go all in and live a life together.
They would raise their kids, work real jobs and live happily ever after.
Here she was on probation still because she copped to a possessions charge, but for him she would play the hand that was dealt.

Majors would have taken a bullet for Terrance if it meant he would be spared.
Because this was her man and has been since she was thirteen.
But she was hot to trot and loved a man with sagging jeans.

Terrance had that D-Boy persona and he had Haughville on lock.
Indianapolis's West side was good to him; he stayed posted up on the block.
Popeye's chicken on west 16th street. Was his honey comb hide out.
That's where he met Majors who only stopped in for a pop.
She and her home girls strolled in with short shorts and bra like tops.
They had banging bodies like grown women with the attitude to match.
Majors had on big ghetto ear rings and lip gloss that popped.

Cell phones, pagers, shades and bubble gum that she popped
Majors was loud and boisterous to stay the least.

A little pissed off cause her mother was a straight up a beast.
Although she referred to her with another word beginning with the capital B

Her momma was a trifling chick who never deserved the title parent, or even Mom
So caught up in the street life Majors was growing up all wrong.
But luckily for Majors she was being raised by her grandparents.

Majors mother Wanda thought she was as young as her daughter.
Smoking, drinking, and clubbing, and screwing anybody's father
Heck she would screw the son and his sister too.
She was that chick that you didn't want around your dude.

So you could say Majors had it honest. She certainly learned from the best.
She never learned how to cook, or clean but could roll a blunt with the finest.
French manicured tips to split the swisher down the middle.
Ready to fill it with that purple haze so she and her girls could get lit

Majors ordered her drink while Terrance watched from the corner of the store.
The smell of chicken in the air and napkins all over the floor
He whispers to his homeboy D-Nut who stood to the right
"Go tell Shorty to come holla at your boy".
D-nut says "aight".

So after getting Majors attention he says "a yo my guy is digging you".
With the tip of her shades she replied, "Who dude"?
Ah yea, that's what's up
Tell him give me a minute
And let me finish up".
"Cool", responds D-Nut as he strolled back to Terrance who was still posted up.
Majors high-fived her friend and she prepared herself to say what's up.

After a few minutes she strolled over his way,
Hand on her hip ready to hear what he had to say.
Terrance smiled at Majors and asked, "Where her man was at"?
She replied, "He's wherever your girl is at
Probably keeping her company
Where you should be at"

Terrance smiles and says, "Fair enough Lil Mama I like your style.
I like what I see, and with me is where you should be".
As she shifts legs from the left one to the right,
She removes her shades and bats her long eyelashes and responds,
"Is that right"?

They exchanged small pleasantries and did a whole lot of flirting.
After exchanging names and numbers they planned to hook up later.
Majors and her buddies dipped out while laughing and joking.

Rochelle asked Majors, "Now why you lie about you age"?
Talking about you seventeen"
"Because he was fine as hell", she replied, besides," I couldn't tell him
I was only thirteen".

Rochelle said. "Like wow you gone get dude caught up"
Majors was like "oh well,
He probably won't even last a month".
"By then I be done put a dent in his pockets he gone throw the number away
But if your girl is lucky I won't be able to keep him away".

Rochelle laughed at Majors because she knew she was for real.
Majors had a heck of a way of thinking crazy.
Under the ghettofied notion of keeping it real
Terrance tells D-Nut "Imma drop you off at the spot in a minute
And hook up with Lil mama and roll on down to Tibbs
So we can watch a movie at the DRIVE-IN".

The Essence Of A Virtuous Woman

D-Nut responds, "Okay that's what's up
Shorty got a helluva body so you know what's up".
Terrance was like "yea you already know
Got to put Shorty to the test and hopefully separate her from the hoes".

You see anytime Terrance and his crew met a new chick,
They had certain things they would do
In order to see if,
She was a keeper or somebody they could run through.

If she gave up the panties on the first date
Then they called her a hoe and treated her as such.
But if she made him wait then they would respect her the next day.
They needed to know if they were dealing with a chick
That had low self-esteem and no respect for herself.
Cause then she would allow them to post up in their cribs all night.

Before you knew it they would be cooking crack in her kitchen
And serving stings from the back door
A real woman would set boundaries and not allow
That kind of crap through her door

Terrance respected a woman who had standards and pride about herself.
A woman who knew her worth and wouldn't settle for less
But with Majors he wasn't sure exactly where she would fall.
She was still young and impressionable so she could be taught to handle it all.

She could possibly be his ride or die because she was straight hood.
And had an attitude that matched he could,
Teach her how to trap and help get her money up.
They would be the Bonny and Clyde of Nap.

So later on Terrance swooped Majors up
Took her to the DRIVE-IN as he promised
And of course she was decked out in her cute Gucci fit.

Her girl Candice stole for her last week at the outlet.

They talked and laughed while watching a movie
The more Terrance listened the more he saw Majors was cool.
He was thinking to himself yea she is a keeper
Just as long as she makes me wait.
To run up in her but then that will change her fate.

Because as of right now he labeled her as a keeper
Majors had no clue she was even being tested.
It's a good thing that she was playing hard to get
Her grandma taught her to make a man wait.

"The more you hold out and keep your candy in the dish.
Men will respect you and whatever you want, they will get".
"Don't no man want a woman he can't take home to his Mama.
So you respect yourself enough to make him wait.
And you will avoid all the drama".

That's what her Grandma used to tell her
Since her Mama was not around.
She relied on the wisdom from the old schools
Past down

Now of course Terrance tried his best
To get in Majors pants but she refused to let,
Him get close enough to even sneak in a kiss.
She made him stay on his side of the car
While she enjoyed the movie from afar.

After the movie they grabbed a bite to eat
Then walked the canal and talked some more he was so intrigued.

Showed her the time of her life too
Spoiled her from that moment on there was nothing he wouldn't do.
Now let's fast forward to this present day in time.
After being together for all this time Terrance has finally lost his mind.

Now Majors is getting calls on her private cell phone.
From women claiming to have kids by the man who just bought her a home
This chick say she been with Terrance for about three years.
And between the two of them they have four kids.

She is trying to check Majors as if she was his wife
But Majors shares a home with him, and he in bed with her every night.
Now granted there have been a few times where he claims he was working late
But he never stayed gone for more than a day.

The stuff this chick was spitting just wasn't adding up.
But she didn't want to give her name and kept calling private
Majors decided to sit back and let the situation play out.
Terrance knew not to play with her cause she was passed cussing him out.

It's been plenty of time when Majors went upside his head.
Trying to play her to the left like some Lil Tramp.
She had the ring the cars and house
Heck she had his heart.
But she wasn't a punk by no means and was gone make that clear.
Just as soon as she got home to hear
What Terrance had to say about these kids.

So of course Terrance denied it all with a straight face
Majors told him, "If I catch you cheating it's a wrap
You will find you another place".

He told her, "she was tripping and to just calm down".
She reminded him, "of all they been through and that she held him down
If she found out there were kids when he had the chance to tell her
He would need more than the Maury show to determine paternity"

He insisted, "That it's just some jealous chick who wants to take
her spot".
"Well how did she get my number"? Majors responded.
Terrance said, "Heck if I know probably from your page
On Facebook "
So Majors left it alone and went into the kitchen to cook.

After dinner Terrance says, "Yo babe I gotta step out".
Majors was like, "ok when will you be back"?
He replies, "just as soon as I handle my business"
She says, "Ok be safe".
And soon as she heard the garage door closed
She was out the door right behind him through the back gate.

She jumped in the rental car she had parked in back of the garage.
And followed him through Castleton heading west on 86th street.
He made a left onto Michigan Road and a right on 71st street.

She followed about 3 cars behind him so he couldn't see
Her ducked off behind the tents of the 2015 Chevy
They just passed Georgetown road when her cell phone rang
The caller ID read private so Majors said, "hello"

The voice on the other end told her what she needed to hear.
Said, "Terrance was on his way over to her crib.
And if Majors didn't believe her then she could join the party".
Since she had a life with the man who was also her kid's father"

Majors stayed on the phone and just listened with content.
And watched her man pull up into a driveway
Leading to the house just left of them.
The chick who answered the door was much older than her.
She watched her man kiss her on the lips as he walked through the
door.

The mystery lady replies, "Ok chick I gotta go
My man just walked through the door so
I will talk to you later when he leaves to go to work
Besides the kids will be gone all weekend with the church".

Majors listened closely because the mystery woman never pressed end.
She could hear the whole conversation between her and her man.
She could hear the giggling and laughing and then kissing
Finally she heard moaning and groaning and that did it.

Why on earth would this chick play this kind of game?
She called Terrance on his cell just to see if he would answer.
And sure enough he said, "Hello" and all out of breath
Majors asked him, "Why he was sounding like that"?
He replied, "Because I ran to grab my phone,
Baby you know I know your ring tone"
She asked. "How soon can you get home"?

He responded, "In a few hours I had to handle some things".
She says, "I bet you do" and then hung up phone.
Mad at the fact it was so easy for him to lie.
She made up in her mind that she would stay posted up outside.

It's now after 1 a.m. and he was still with her laid up.
She finally got up enough nerve to walk up.
To the windows to peek through
They were getting busy right in the living room.
She could see her sitting on her man's lap.
Having a good old time butt naked

As she glanced around the room she could see pictures hanging on the wall
Some with little boys and little girls but this one topped it all
It was her with a wedding gown on and guess who was the groom?
Mr. Terrance of course he was holding the broom.

That they apparently jumped over on their wedding day
But this picture looks recent because he just started growing his dreads.
He has always been the type to sport a faded head.
Just the thought of it all had Majors mad as can be.
She said to herself Imma teach him not to mess with me.

She got a cup from the car and posted up on the porch.
Dropped her drawls and squatted over the cup
She released her bowels that her stomach in knots
And took a tinkle in the driveway up to the house

She began to bang on the door and when they looked out
She dumped the cup of dung all over the porch.
She grabbed the can of gasoline from the trunk of the car.
And began pouring it on the chairs on the porch
And the windshield of his car

He could see her from the bay window in the front
Freaking out cause he knew what she was capable of.
The wife or baby mama whatever you want to call her
Screamed, "She was calling the police".
Majors responded, now why you wanna go and do that?
Remember you invited me so let's party"!

"Either you send Terrance out or y'all gone both go up in flames.
Since he want to keep lying, and you playing these childish games
Terrance should have told you that I am not the one.
You don't want to go toe to toe with me because you will lose every time.

So she tells Terrance, "He better get his fling.
Because clearly she is the one wearing his ring"
Truthfully Terrance was scared because Majors was a different kind of crazy.
She was the type that would set the house on fire with both of them in it.

He came out the house and stepped right in her dung.
Immediately he regretted even answering his phone.
He had been in a relationship with both women for years
The wife knew about Majors but Majors had no clue.

So after fighting with Terrance and trying to set him on fire

The Essence Of A Virtuous Woman

The neighbors finally called the cops.
And she was locked up for domestic violence
And attempted Arson

Terrance bonded her out and came clean about everything.
He says to Majors, "dig this here me and my wife used to swing.
This is why she didn't have a problem with me seeing you".
Majors was still in shock and mad as hell.
Wishing he would have just left her locked up in that cell.

In a matter of moments her whole world crashed.
In love with a man who was full of games
She gave him her life at an early age.

Unsure of how she would deal
Had her crying uncontrollably until, she took a handful of pills
And laid down so she could take an eternal sleep
But just as she was dozing off
She could see.

Her best friend Rochelle at the foot of her bed
Crying and asking what had she done?
When Rochelle heard what she did at Terrance house,
She had dozed off waiting at Majors crib on the couch.

She heard her come in but wanted to give her time to settle in.
She didn't want her friend to be alone so when,
She thought she would go in to check on her.
She saw her limped body and the empty pill bottle.

She called the paramedics and stayed on the phone while she waited
Fussing at her friend for doing something so stupid
She rushed her to the hospital, where the Dr. pumped her stomach
Cleared all the traces of ibuprofen

Majors stayed on suicide watch for a while.
With Rochelle at her bedside the whole time

She expressed to Majors that she should have never put her hope in
a man
And if you wanted to then she had a man that she could
recommend.

A Man who will love her and treat her like queen
And through faith and hope in Him
She could have anything.

Rochelle shared the good news about Jesus Christ.
Prayed for her and Majors asked Him
To come into her life
And make everything that she had been going through alright.

Now Majors and Rochelle are active in church.
In the youth Ministry department of all places
Majors shares her testimony as often as she can.
Inspiring young ladies to wait on the man

That God has ordained to be in their lives.
To focus on school and grades and enjoying life
She is encouraging them to stay pure and practice abstinence.
She wanted to be the one to share her testimony.
And to make a difference in the lives of others

The girls get a kick of how crazy she was.
But she explained, "That when in love
With a man who didn't love me,
Made it really easy for him to make
A complete fool out of me"

She said, "I never would have guessed in a million years
That Terrance would have been the reason behind so many of my
tears.
I had caught a drug case all in the name of love.
Got locked up for domestic violence
And even tried to take my own life
All behind a man playing games with my heart".

"So please take your time and don't rush
Sex and relationships can all wait.
Cause when you are a teenager
Everything sounds good
These men prey on your emotions".

"But you don't have to end up like me". She said
"You all have a bright future ahead.
Just use good judgment and value
Yourselves
There is not a man on this earth worth the pain that I felt.
I want to see you ladies excel at all you do
Although I'm not saying you can't find real love in the hood.
My prayer is that you love God first, and then loving yourself will
be a breeze.
So when true love finds you,
Then you can fall in happily with ease.

I SEE

It's so amazing that when I look into your eyes I see potential, I see pride. I see the man God created you to be,
I see the man who truly has the potential to love me, and women who look like me.

I see a man of strength, a man of character and poise.
I see the struggle of a man that deserves to be loved.
I see creativity and stubbornness as well.
I see sexiness and style, a man who can keep the secrets I choose to tell.

I see humility and courage and swag as big as the sea.
I see a man who has the ability to truly care for me, my babies, and the community.
I see a father who is crazy about his kids.
I see an amazing son with compassion for his mother.
I see a man who likes to inspire other kids.

I see an amazing brother who has his sisters back.
I see an uncle to a niece who doesn't know the meaning of lack.
I see a man whose heart has been broken; I sense the tears that have been shed, without words ever being spoken.

I see a man who is inquisitive and truly desires to the know truth.
To have faith in God and understand his own truths
I see a man that's been predestined for greatness, a man whose future is so bright; you need shades just to see it.

I see a man full of romance, and intimacy.
A man tired of watching his people suffer from senseless acts of violence.
I see a man that has overcome a lot in his past and present.
A man who could use a woman in his life as a companion
I see a man who can be over protective at times, although I see greatness you could use a little time to unwind.

The Essence Of A Virtuous Woman

I see a man who desires a change, but doesn't know how to begin.
I see a man so used to losing he doesn't know how it feels to actually win.
I see a man who deserves the fruits of God's Spirit through and through.
I see a man that God told all Power and authority has been given unto you.

I see a man who I wish could finally see what I see.
and understand the true meaning and value of sight
not from the natural standpoint but spiritual viewpoint
and recognize His God given rights.

God has given you dominion over everything He has called you to do and be.
The same power that raised Jesus Christ from the grave
Is the exact same power that resides within you and me

I see strength and power and I call you blessed.
I call you forth for a time such as this.
Our daughters need you!
Our son's need you!
Our school's need you!
Our churches and communities need you!
Our nations need you!

I see beauty in my Black man,
My African man
My brother man
My friend
My HUMAN
We Love you MAN!

I see you walking in your purpose,
Believing in your destiny,
Changing lives and raising families.
I see you happy, Do you?

Mary Magdalene

It was right here this was the very spot
Where I saw Him look, I know it sounds crazy
At least that's what they thought.

The others seem to think I was losing my mind.
Heck I almost believed them too
Until I remembered all things that I used to do

I know who I used to be.
That is before He found me
Possessed, insane yeah I was crazy
But He healed me.

I'm not imagining this, it was early this morning
It all happened like this.
Before dawn, we came to the tomb with burial spices and such.
But when we got here, there were no guards, no stone, not a body
There was really not much.

We thought His body must have been stolen
His mother wept.
The other women took off running for help.
I stumbled into the garden wondering who could have done such a thing.
Who in the world could have been so mean?

That's when I heard His voice.
I tell you I heard him call my name.
"Mary," Just like a hundred times before
It's always been the same.
Without thinking I turned but then I remembered He was gone.
After being crucified on the cross and for so long

I saw someone standing there "help me"! I cried
Do you know where they've taken our Lord and why?

And again I heard it "Mary"
He called me by my name.

As the first rays of sunlight crept across the sky
The horizon was beautiful in my eyes.
They fell on the stranger and in the light I could see his face
I looked into His eyes.

The face of our Lord
He spoke to me by name.
He said, "To find the disciples
And tell them I came".

It's not my imagination I'm certainly not crazy.
I saw him and he spoke to me.
So no matter how it seems
No matter what anyone says?
I know Jesus is alive
He has risen and is still alive today.

This poem is dedicated to Mrs. JoAnne Davis-Jones with the W.I.N.G.S. Ministry of Mt. Ararat Baptist Church located in Houston Texas. I performed this poem as part of a stage play entitled He Is Risen. Which depicted the moments of resurrection of Jesus Christ from Mary Magdalene's standpoint. This play was written and directed by JoAnne and I must say she is brilliant. I look forward to working with her in the future. This scene has been re-worded by Bridgette Thornton to put it in poetic form and featured in this book with the verbal permission of Mrs. JoAnne Davis-Jones.

Excerpts from The UnMasking Of Me
Written by: Bridgette Thornton

THE UNMASKING OF ME

It's been kind of difficult in my search to find me:
Having to face my life's most challenging difficulties,
Trying to find the balance and place where I begin
Knowing my life has a purpose, with very little room for sin.

Having lots of unanswered questions about my past,
That's still affecting my future today.
Living with the consequences of decisions that I've made:

The entire time God was perfecting me for His pleasure alone:
So the physical, mental, and sexual abuse, were the foundation of my home.
Those experiences painted the perfect picture of what I didn't want to be.
So I had to protect and encourage my beautiful babies.

Not realizing that bondage had a hold on me.
Making it extremely difficult, to chastise my babies
I felt the need to shower them with so much unconditional love,
By giving them the knowledge of God's word: with His unchanging love.

Now I know somewhere along this path I've said and done some things,
That I can't take back today.
So I apologize, from the bottom of my heart but what can I say?

Just know I have been held accountable for all mistakes I've made.
I have asked God for forgiveness, each and every day.
So with The Unmasking of Me, I shed plenty of tears.

I had to come face to face, with some of my greatest fears.

In this journey I found out that not everyone loved me.
So I had to find that love in God, who truly loves me.
I had to pray and ask God to teach me how to be,
The woman of God that He created me to be:

I had to make myself available to receive His precious word.
By fasting and worshiping. And spreading His word,
Satan has no dominion in my life at all,
For I am a child of God and on His word I'll stand tall:
He thought he had me with the molestation as a child,
He just knew that with the pain and rejection I felt that
I would go wild.

But sense that didn't work, then suicide should have been a sure win.
But God had angels surrounding me, and protecting me even back then
Let's not forget about the physical abuse
That they labeled whooping's Unable to sit for days,
Because my bottom was still healing from the bruising

But by God's stripes I was healed and made whole.
For a time such as this, for my story to be told:
The testimony of a great work God has done in me.
By mending the broken heart, I blamed on my family.

Because even in my marriage Satan thought he had a chance.
I just knew my husband had been sexually active with another man.
But even in my sin I wouldn't dare agree with that.
A perverse spirit had him under attack.
But had I been praying back then the abuse may have ceased.
And my home would have been filled with joy and lots of peace.

Since God orchestrates all things?
He has had His hand on my life because He is the almighty King.
So if all things work together for my good since the
Lord is who I truly serve.

*Then cover me in the blood of Jesus because that's the only blood
that saves.*

*However through all of this mess,
God found a reason for me to be blessed.
He gave me three beautiful souls that I have the liberty to raise.
He's mended the torn relationship with my Mom, we talk every
day.*

*He's placed me in a circle of people you may call my friends,
I call them protecting angles that God is using to mend.
Those torn places in my past by making memories for right now,
By encouraging and motivating me to be proud.*

*Of the new me that God has under construction,
I'm definitely a work in progress but far from self-destruction.
By attempting to live this life, according to God's perfect will.
By knowing my responsibility as a believer I still,*

*Have the right to speak things that are not, as though they were,
Because they are:
I'm the head and not the tail, so by faith I will go far.*

*God has blessed me with my business, my children have one too.
I plan to leave an inheritance, as the word says to do.
I acknowledge Him in all things, in spirit and in truth.
I try to learn from my mistakes and allow myself to be used.*

*By God on each and every day to show myself approved
I start with The Unmasking of Me
So I can do the work God has called me to do.*

FORGIVENESS

Now I must say, well I have to admit,
I've been through some things
That were kind of hard to deal with.
I say this that even right now,
As I think back I try to see how.

How I've made it through this far:
Because it just wasn't fare:
For someone who had been written off
Made to feel as though no one cared:

What I am about to say you may find a little alarming.
However if I could just reach that one somebody
Then the pain that I have suffered
Would not be in vain, but a means to an end
To help them proclaim.

Their victory and take their life back,
From the very offender who had them under attack.
Wow, let's see, where should I begin?
Rather who should I address first?
Let's start with the man, who caused me the most hurt,

I forgive you for sneaking into my room late at night.
For fondling my fragile body, when you knew you weren't right.
I forgive you for forcing yourself inside of me.
For trying to convince my mother I was lying:

I forgive you for making me feel that I had to endure.
Your sick perverted ways that only God could have cured.
I forgive you for your physical, mental and sexual abuse.
For molesting my sister and I, there was simply no excuse.

I forgive you for making me feel dirty.
As if I was the one who was unworthy.

I forgive you for invading that piece of me.
That precious jewel, you took my virginity.

I forgive you because you have made it so difficult for me
But it's all okay.
To truly love a man, and allow God to have his way:
I forgive you for putting me in bondage, but it's safe to say I'm finally free.
Because in forgiving you, I also had to forgive me.

For blaming all of my failed relationships on you:
In doing so I've giving all of the power and glory to you.
But it stops here because only God gets the glory.
This is why I'm finally able to tell my story.

It's too bad that it's taking me so long.
To let go of the hurt and pain from how you treated me so wrong.
I forgive you because now I'm able to actually have
A relationship with my Mom, because now I'm no so mad.

I used to think she was just as wrong as you,
Her job was to protect me from creeps like you.
So not only do I forgive you.
For all of the years of pain:
I thank you for allowing the enemy
To use you for his personal gain:

Because of the abuse I've giving myself such a hard time.
Trying to protect my children at all times
It's too bad that you are already deceased.
I pray you had the chance to go to God for peace.

I pray that you were giving the chance to make things right.
By repenting and asking for the forgiveness in his sight.
For molesting me and my sister and creating the pain that we suffer.
And not just for us but for all of the others.

If for some reason God has sent you straight to hell.

I pray that it is much comfortable then the story I have to tell.
But the good news at the end of the day
I had to experience your abuse, to help show someone else the way.

The moment you give your burdens to God
He'll make your life so bright.
He is the only reason why I live my life.
So yes, you know who you are
No need to say your name aloud,
Because I'm free from your abuse
I no longer wear a frown.

I forgive you this you must know,
But instead I make it my business
To let the parents know.
The signs of a child's depression
Caused by sexual molestation:

Nothing is too hard for God
This I know for a fact.
Everything you lose to the enemy
I guarantee God gives it all back.

All things work together for the good
Of those who love the Lord Just like me.
So only He will get the glory,
So yes I forgive you, as I tell my story.

Bridgette N. Thornton

IMPORTANT SCRIPTURES TO KNOW WHAT THE BIBLE HAS TO SAY

COMFORT WHEN FEELING DEPRESSED

1. PSALM   27
2. PSALM   9-9
3. PSALM   18-2
4. PSALM   22-24
5. PSALM   23
6. PSALM   27.4-5
7. PSALM   30-5
8. ISAIAH   66.12-14

STRENGTH WHEN YOU ARE WEAK

1. MATTHEW   11. 25-30
2. JOHN   14. 1-4
3. JOHN   14-27
4. ROMANS 8 31-39
5. PSALM   18 1-3
6. 1 CHRONICLES   16-11
7. NEMEMIAH   8-10
8. PSALM   27-1

FORGIVENESS

1. NUMBERS   14. 19-21
2. MICAH   7.18-19
3. MATTHEW   5-24
4. MATTHEW   5. 44-45
5. MATTHEW   6. 9-15
6. MATTHEW   18. 21-35
7. MARK   11-25
8. LUKE   6. 35-38 42

WOMEN STRUGGLING WITH SELF ESTEEM ISSUES

1. *PROVERBS 31. 10-31*
2. *1 JOHN 3-1*
3. *ROMANS 3-23*
4. *MATTHEW 11. 28-30*
5. *GENESIS 1. 26-27*
6. *JOSHUA 1-9*
7. *ROMANS 15-4*
8. *EPHESIANS 6-13*

LOVE~ LOVE ~ LOVE~ LOVE

1. *1 CORITHIANS 13. 4-7*
2. *JOHN 3-16*
3. *JOHN 13-35*
4. *NUMBERS 14-17*
5. *1 CORITHIANS 13-13*
6. *MARK 12-31*
7. *JOHN 14-16*
8. *GALATIONS 5-22*

FAITH

1. *PROVERBS 3-5-6*
2. *HEBREWS 11-1*
3. *HEBREWS 11-6*
4. *EPHESIANS 2-8*
5. *2 CORITHIANS 5-7*
6. *ROMANS 1-17*
7. *MATTHEW 17-20*
8. *LUKE 7-50*

FASTING

1. *ISAIAH 58-6*
2. *MATTHEW 6. 16-18*

3. ACTS 14-23
4. ACTS 13-12
5. ESTHER 4-16
6. DANIEL 9-3
7. MATTHEW 4-4
8. JONAH 3.5-10

ABUSE AND OVERCOMING IT

1. JAMES 5-16
2. GALATIONS 5. 19-21
3. 1 CORITHIANS 6. 9-20
4. ROMANS 1. 26-27
5. 1 TIMOTHY 1. 9-11
6. MATTHEW 18-6
7. LUKE 6-27
8. TITUS 3-5

VICTORY

1. 1 CORITHIANS 10-13
2. DEUTERONOMY 20-4
3. 1 PETER 3-18
4. JAMES 1.12-14
5. 2 CORITHIANS 12. 9-10
6. PSALM 108-13
7. JOHN 16-33
8. PHILIPIANS 4-13

FOR WISDOM AND UNDERSTANDING

BOOK OF PROVERBS

FOR PRAYER, PRAISE AND WORSHIP

BOOK OF PSALM

LOVE

GALATIONS

WHAT THE BIBLE SAYS ABOUT RAPE
GENESIS 34

Important numbers that may help to save a life.

All information on this page is public information and can be obtained from any search engine such as Yahoo or Google. For additional information, assistance, resources, and community connections you can always use the following:

9-1-1 Emergency
4-1-1- Directory Assistance
2-1-1 Community Assistance

National Suicide prevention lifeline number
1-800-273-8255
www.suicidepreventionlifeline.org 24/7
For help, they assist individuals in the United States in a crisis situation contact the nearest prevention specialist in your area.

National Domestic Violence Hotline *1-800-799-7233*
www.thehotline.org 24/7
For assistant with a highly trained advocate who's available to assist you with seeking resources or information and answer questions about unhealthy relationships, and domestic violence.

National Aids Hotline *1-800-232-4636*
Centers for Disease Control and Prevention
www.cdc.org
One stop shop for all the information and resources you need to know about testing sites and updated information for your zip code.

About The Author

Bridgette Thornton was born and raised in Indianapolis Indiana to Bridgette Wallace and dearly departed Richard Lee Thornton. She resided in Houston Texas for 7 years before returning back home to Indy to further her career while being close to family and friends. She is also the proud parent of three extraordinary children Kamaria (16) KamRon (12) Kaiden (9).

Bridgette is also the Founder and CEO to **Divas in Red Outreach Ministry Inc.**, **NuAge Job Readiness Program Inc**. and Co-Founder to **Trio K Kids Kandy LLC**. Also the author to The UnMasking of Me. Bridgette is very active in her community through her Non-Profit organization Divas In Red Outreach Ministry Inc. She has had the pleasure of working with teen age girls between the ages of 12 and 17 as a mentor, educator, and role model and motivational Speaker. Focusing on teaching them to be women of God through hands on activities to learn more about how to get involved and see the lives that are being changed you can visit www.divasinredindy.org.

Through NuAge Job Readiness Program Inc. she assists individuals in need of employment by assisting them with resume building, interviewing techniques, and referrals to companies who are looking to hire. She also assists individuals interested in starting a small business prepare, plan and strategize to become business owners and or better employees.

Bridgette's love for travel keeps her on the road, ready to meet new people and experience diverse cultures and ways of life. She is a firm believer in giving back as often as possible through her tithes, talents, and tools. Her strong faith in God keeps her pressing forward to greater challenges. She has hope in being married again. She is full of life, love and believes that prayer changes everything but until God shows up to fix the situation you may as well laugh uncontrollably until it gets better.

She is adamant about early education. The more children are taught while they are willing to learn the more things they will retain as adults and prayerfully be able to make a huge difference in a dying world.

Bridgette is an advocate against domestic violence, black on black crime and child abuse. These things are important to her because it hinders one's ability to live, love, laugh and grow spiritually economically and socially. No one has the right to hurt or harm another human being rather it is physically, mentally, or sexually. We all have the right to live, and to live in peace.

PHOTO GALLERY
Virtuous Women

BRIDGETTE THORNTON

In this section of this book you will see photos and names of a few women in my life whom I have nominated as being Virtuous Women. You may not get to read their stories, or see their names in bright lights, but to me, they shine brighter than any star you will ever see in the sky. These women are WARRIORS, SURVIVORS, CHAMPIONS, SUPERHEROS, most of all, my absolute favorite, My Guardian Angels. They are my Inspiration. That's why I wanted to take a moment to celebrate these Virtuous Women in all of their Essence.

ADRIENNE HUDSON

ELFREDA DYCUS

Bridgette N. Thornton

KAMARIA THORNTON-FORD

BRIDGETTE WALLACE

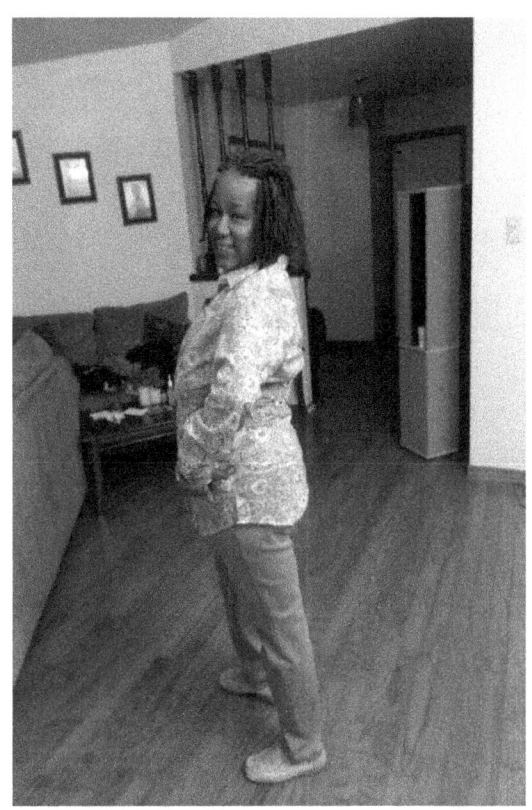

FALISHA BRIGHTWELL

KIZZY HAYES

MELISSA JONES

The Essence Of A Virtuous Woman

GINA SCOTT-HAWKINS

KIANA FOSSETT

The Essence Of A Virtuous Woman

ROTUNDA HAYES-MONTGOMERY

ROCHELLE THORNTON

SHEMEKA CORNETT

Bridgette N. Thornton

www.ingramcontent.com/pod-product-compliance
Lightning Source LLC
Chambersburg PA
CBHW070500100426
42743CB00010B/1701